The Ethics of Teaching at Sites of Violence and Trauma

Natalie Bormann

The Ethics of Teaching at Sites of Violence and Trauma

Student Encounters with the Holocaust

Natalie Bormann
Department of Political Science
Northeastern University
Boston, MA, USA

ISBN 978-1-137-59444-0   ISBN 978-1-137-59445-7   (eBook)
DOI 10.1057/978-1-137-59445-7

Library of Congress Control Number: 2017950667

Cover illustration: Abstract Bricks and Shadows © Stephen Bonk/Fotolia.co.uk

Printed on acid-free paper

This Palgrave Macmillan imprint is published by Springer Nature
The registered company is Nature America Inc.
The registered company address is: 1 New York Plaza, New York, NY 10004, U.S.A.

"Last night I dreamt I was a suitcase. A suitcase of a girl I don't know. Filled carefully with all that she found precious, made whole by carrying her life. Carried closely to her body, and held tightly to her chest. She placed me down delicately, remembering where she had left me. Then I was flying through the air. Ripped open as her life escaped my careful hands. Everything that she had put inside me vanished into the property of history. Empty and stripped I was left alone, as was she. More suitcases piled upon me as those piled upon her because like her I was small and fragile. Suffocated by the emptiness I lay there for an eternity as more and more fell on top of me, the burden too heavy, the load too empty."
(Student reflection on our visit to Auschwitz-Birkenau)

PREFACE

This book completes a period of just over four consecutive years during which I developed, and then lead, a Holocaust study abroad program. My experience and observations while leading this program provide the context for reflection on fundamental issues and challenges of Holocaust education at sites of trauma and violence. Each summer, this program takes a group of twenty dedicated undergraduate students from across campus of a private, New England, University on a five-week long journey through Germany and Poland—two countries, five cities, four concentration camps, all day visits to Auschwitz, workshops, seminars, memorials, museums, documentation centers, former ghettos, talks with survivors; the list goes on.

Two political science-based courses (four credit points each) provide the backbone for this experiential program; one of the courses is designed to introduce students to the political and historical context of the Holocaust through the lens of the concepts of totalitarianism, fascism, sovereign power, and the categories of perpetrators, victims, and bystanders. The other course aims at exploring the role of trauma, memory, and ethics in the practices of commemoration, remembrance, and forgetting; prompting a critical understanding of the relevance of the Holocaust for the prevention of genocides today. Taken together, both elements zoom in on questions of why and how it was possible to commit these mass atrocities, before thinking about how and to what effect current and future societies are informed and educated about the Holocaust.

The program is "busy," to put it mildly. Students fulfill *all* their credit requirements while traveling in form of classic, research, and reflection papers based on the activities on the ground, and accompanied by a selection of reading material. There are four components to the entire program: an application process that includes a one-on-one interview with students wishing to participate. This is followed by three group orientation sessions, the travel to Europe, and lastly, a follow-up session with oral and written feedback opportunities. The encounters narrated here draw from all of these components.

The story of this book neither began with a particular theory or expertise about Holocaust education in general, nor with a deep knowledge of the concept of a Holocaust study abroad program in particular. Rather, it came to be through a series of, maybe innocent yet somewhat memorable, encounters. By encounters I mean moments when my participant observations about, and with, my group of students seemed to repeatedly illustrate for me the ethical complexities latent in the process of teaching at sites of trauma—the complexities of "being-there" (at sites of trauma and violence). This book takes these personal notes and uses them to query existing paradigms and larger narratives of Holocaust education.

Some preliminary thoughts on this book's aim and scope are in order. The aim is twofold; on the one hand, I try to synthesize a concrete experiential teaching account with pressing, contemporary debates on Holocaust education. On the other hand, I offer a critical assessment of the ethical concerns we are confronted with when learning at sites of trauma and suffering. Ultimately, at least in my mind, this book is driven by my search for a more ethically perceptive model for learning and teaching about the Holocaust in particular, and atrocities in general.

Boston, USA   Natalie Bormann

Acknowledgements

This book would not have been possible without the wonderful students at Northeastern University in Boston, USA, with whom I have been spending my summers teaching at sites of trauma and violence in Germany and Poland. Their inquisitive minds, resilience, and open hearts are what fuels my passion for teaching; their courage to confront the atrocities of the Holocaust keeps inspiring me in continuing with this study abroad program. Three students stand out in particular—Ellen Callahan, Amanda Knightly, and Helen Sattler—who provided some essential preliminary research on some of the encounters that are narrated here. I am also indebted to my colleagues who assisted me in organizing this program—in the USA as well as abroad. Veronica Czastkiewicz has been an integral part in bringing this program to life, and we have since then written about our experiences as coauthors.[1] Those who hosted my students year after year across Germany and Poland; the incredibly welcoming individuals—you know who you are—and their respective institutions, many of which are featured in this book. The project itself was framed and researched during a generous 2015 Jack and Anita Hess Seminar follow-up grant with the Jack, Josep and Morton Mandel Center for Advanced Holocaust Studies at the United States Holocaust Memorial Museum in Washington D.C., and with continuous support from my academic home, the Political Science Department at Northeastern. I am grateful to Elizabeth Dauphinee's review comments and constructive suggestions on this project; you steered me into the direction of the concept of haunting which was the missing piece in the framing of my recollection of encounters at sites.

~ *Gegen das Vergessen* ~

NOTE

1. Bormann, N. and Czastkiewicz, V. (2017) '"Postcard from Auschwitz?": Chronicling the Challenges of a Holocaust Study Abroad Program', in Budryte, D. and Boykin, S. (Eds.) *Engaging Difference. Teaching Humanities and Social Science in Multicultural Environments*, (Rowman & Littlefield), pp. 111–120.

CONTENTS

CHAPTER 1

The Problem with *"Being There"*

Abstract Student visits to sites of trauma and violence are fundamentally based on the promise that there is an educational value of "being there"; a direct encounter with history through seeing, hearing, and feeling. Over the course of three years of leading a Holocaust study abroad program, my observations would certainly align with the expectation of such promise. However, and as existing research shows, it is not often clear what the exact value, impact, or takeaway in fact is—or ought to be. Through an exploration of the opportunities and limits of visiting sites of trauma with groups of students, and here through the lens of the encounters with my own cohorts, I suggest that the first step to a deep engagement with historic sites and museums must be to prompt students to decode the ethical complexities of self-reflexivity, visual literacy, and the politics of spectatorship.

Keywords Ethics · Being there · Experiential education Autoethnography

How are we supposed to reflect on, learn, and teach about events that we never experienced directly? As educators, we often assume the answer lies in the concept of "being there": The notion of experiencing history—through a direct encounter with the sites where history took place, and by way of seeing, hearing, and feeling.[1] Intimacy with the material, so the argument goes, facilitates interest, authenticates knowledge, and

© The Author(s) 2018   1
N. Bormann, *The Ethics of Teaching at Sites of Violence and Trauma,*
DOI 10.1057/978-1-137-59445-7_1

produces venues for personal growth and reflection—all of which promises to ensure a deep, personal engagement that is not only to stay with the learner but is also said to nurture ethical thinking, generate empathy, and reconfigure a person's worldview.[2]

Much of this goes back to Dewey's seminal and much quoted work on experiential education that tasks educators with creating opportunities for students to "actively engage in the learning process," and with providing hands-on, intentional experiences.[3] Holocaust education is perhaps at the forefront of implementing ideas of experiential learning in an attempt to engage students in more meaningful, interested, and purposeful ways—outside the classroom. Such opportunities are realized most fundamentally through the experience at the physical structures of historical sites that were once central to the organization and execution of the Holocaust. Scholars agree that the built environment, geography, ruins, and artefacts are powerful in augmenting other, existing, forms of methodology and analysis, namely narrative history or visual representations.[4]

The encounters with my students at historical sites of trauma and violence, chronicled here, seem to suggest likewise; to begin with, there is indeed a widespread desire by the learner for experiencing and "living history," whereby a past and otherwise distant event such as the Holocaust can somehow be folded into a personal and local memory.[5] *"Being there brought it home for me,"* is certainly one of the most popular expressions among my traveling students over the course of three years of leading a Holocaust study abroad program to Europe. This experience often culminated for the students in the visit to Auschwitz:

> Auschwitz was important to see. It made me really think about the victims, it broke down the number barrier of not being able to fathom what eleven million people is. I can envision it now.

One of the curators at the Auschwitz Memorial Museum endorses the uniqueness of the experience of "being there" during our visit by stating: *"People come here to feel it, touch it, experience it."*

When I first began thinking about developing a Holocaust study abroad program I was already invested—personally and academically—in the phenomenon of memorials and museum sites as spaces of understanding and remembering the past; the ways in which memorials and museums are "at work" and attract millions of people, or, more precisely, tourists; the ways in which societies such as mine (German) are continuously imbued with performances of remembrance and commemoration at those sites; and the ways in which those sites grapple with this interplay of practices of remembering and forgetting, of warning and teaching, of preserving and altering historical memory. How can it be that former killing sites such as Auschwitz-Birkenau attract millions of people each year?

Most fundamentally, "being there" is said to assist in, literally, envisaging the depth (and scale) of the event.[6] Students report, for instance, that seeing the large area of Auschwitz-Birkenau and *"the immense collection of personal items, family photos, portraits, clothes"* assists them to *"imagine the scale"* of systemic mass violence. With that come specific sensory features that accompany space—smells, sounds, and images.[7] Some students claim to notice that the lavatories in the old barracks at Auschwitz-Birkenau *"still smell like human feces,"* or simply that *"the sky was gray"* matching the *"solemnness of the day,"* adding to their memory of the suffering endured at these sites.

More importantly—at least for me—are the accidental experiences of "being there"; the things one cannot—but would *expect* to see; or the things one notices but would *not expect* to see. One student describes such an experience when approaching the site of Dachau: *"the first thing that shocked me was the fact that there were residential areas so close to the memorial site of the camp."* Such reflections complicate for students the ways in which they structure their knowledge of the Holocaust. In this case, it unsettles the often neat and tidy categorization of perpetrators, victims, witnesses, and bystanders; the lines between these actors become blurred. We meet residents of the town of Dachau whose balconies overlook the site of the former concentration camp; they tell my students that moving to the town of Dachau was for economic reasons—housing is much more affordable here for a family of four than in Munich, leaving an imprint with my cohort on the concepts of memory, forgetting, and moving on that cannot be gained in any meaningful way outside this personal encounter at the site. One of the most common reflections on the program is aptly described by one student as the importance of *"seeing shades of grey."*

"Being *there*" (as opposed to *"here"* at home) means also that students often assume different identities, roles, and responsibilities. Students notice that they take on the different perspectives of local communities and experts (like the families of Dachau with whom they find themselves sympathizing), and that they are confronted with scenarios, questions, and approaches to learning about the Holocaust that only reveal themselves by being at the sites, places, and cities themselves. Students reflect on their role as global citizens with an awareness of conflicts today; as one student commented: "*the world and conflicts make more sense to me now that I exposed myself to the Holocaust.*"

Yet, how such encounters with past human suffering at sites are to be accomplished and structured exactly, what the modes of "seeing, hearing, and feeling" of experiential learning ought to be, and what these experiences ultimately culminate to, is less clear. What should and should not, or can and cannot be seen, heard, and viewed? When is the exposure to the material on site perhaps *too* intimate, too emotional? How far is the role of the educator imbued in creating a productive encounter for the learner—and to what effect? And lastly, what exactly is being brought home? What kind of knowledge is being incubated by the cohort, and how the experiences of "being there" translate into concrete opportunities for attitude and activity today, is certainly less agreed upon.

The purpose of this book is not, and cannot be, to fill that gap by producing empirical data on the ways in which teaching my students at sites of trauma can yield specific, measurable, outcomes. Instead, the collection of stories and observations here seek to foreground those very moments when the value and impact of "being there" was rendered most challenging for me as an educator. I argue that this shift in focus has the potential to illuminate and query some of the assumptions we make regarding Holocaust education and its effects. Ultimately, I am interested in tracing an essential question: To what extent may there be a conflict between our ethical imperative to remember a catastrophic past, and the impetus to find ways to teach about it?[8]

THE PROGRAM

Every summer, twenty-five outstanding undergraduate students from across the campus of a private university in the northeast of the USA, travel to Germany and Poland, with the objective to learn about the Holocaust at the very sites where it occurred. We travel for five weeks in two countries and five cities (Munich, Nuremberg, Berlin, Warsaw, Krakow)—destinations that are deemed central to the rise of National Socialism and to the planning and execution of the Holocaust. The group explores three concentration camps (Dachau, Ravensbrück, Sachsenhausen), and spends two days at Auschwitz with an overnight stay adjacent to the death camp. We visit memorials, museums, and documentation centers and participate in workshops, study days, and seminars at those sites, and with support of the educational programs offered on site. Students encounter local communities, experts, and survivors of the Holocaust in structured, as well as unstructured, activities.

Academically and pedagogically, this study abroad program rests on the commitment to what is termed "double attentiveness."[9] The term, invoked by Simon and Eppert in the context of witnessing testimonies and the obligations of the bearer of such witnessing, is composed of two parts, or forms. One part of the attentiveness involves the ability to fold learned and observed information into specific procedures and templates of meaning that validate the historical information. For instance, the ability to recognize information about the structures of concentration camps as part of the strategies of National Socialism, or a fascist ideology. The other involves an ability to honor the specificity of historical information. For instance, the ways in which one remembers, commemorates, and observes that history today.

The commitment to double attentiveness is reflected by the two syllabi that structure the program, and which unquestionably provide the academic backbone of the experience; initially, a Political Science course aims at teaching the politics and history of National Socialism and the Holocaust. Within this context, the group is prompted to think through the political science "lens"—the role of fascism, National Socialism, racism, and anti-Semitism as a political ideology; the role of totalitarianism and absolutism as a systemic problematic; the role of the nation state, the logic of sovereignty, and state-absolved violence as an inherent structural problem; the role of the military and the mobilization of political violence; the role of demagogues and right-wing populism; and the power of resistance and compliance. The purpose is to provide an analytical framework that aids students in making connections between the Holocaust and current, as well as future, genocides. It follows the template of what Simon accentuates as "the enactment of historical memory," which points to the importance of transference of knowledge.[10]

The other course has to do with the role of commemoration—with what happens at sites of memory, with questions of memory, trauma, remembrance, and forgetting. Here, students are provided with the more interpretative frameworks geared toward helping them to engage more critically with the representations of the Holocaust today—the role of museum politics; the politics of memory and trauma; the role of preservation and aesthetization of sites of trauma; and the overall impact of a constantly shifting memorial landscape. Students become aware and reflective of their own role as learners but also as witnesses: I am looking to Simon again who speaks of the importance of the concept of *transitivity*, or, transformative learning, which suggests a focus on "what passes over" and takes effect.[11] Specifically, it signals the importance of thinking through the ways in which learning about the past may offer a real opportunity to live differently in the present. As James Young points out: the importance is not simply how one is moved by historical images and narratives but rather to what end one has been moved in terms of the understanding and actions of one's own life.[12]

Running this program for three years means concretely: Over sixty male and female students, freshmen and seniors alike, have participated and who declared their interest in this program for one or both of the following two reasons:

Curriculum related. Most students apply to the program because of the role the Holocaust plays in their current academic studies. These students major in history, political science, international affairs but also psychology, nursing, and journalism. This also means, there is some foundational knowledge in place with regard to the material covered.

Extracurriculum related. Some students apply for personally motivated reasons; those are either based on a genuine interest in studying the Holocaust outside/or alongside their regular academic studies. This applies especially to students who major in the sciences and for whom this program counts as an elective. "*This program was something I had to do*" responded one student and referring here to a sense of responsibility as a global citizen. In addition, some students are driven by strictly personal and intimate reasons and who see this program as an opportunity to reconnect with their Jewish history and heritage, or German/Polish ancestries.

THE CHALLENGES

The rationale for teaching about the Holocaust is well documented—so are its promises and challenges.[13] The same can be said about the concept of experiential education, within which the study abroad program is couched academically.[14] There are many ways to summarize these promises and challenges, whereby three main categories of complexities, or issue areas, when teaching at sites and museums, can be identified[15]:

To begin with, there are practical issues. For instance, the often physical and emotional demands on students while traveling far away from home (in the case of many, for the first time). In this sense, it is fair to describe this program as both busy and difficult. "Busy" in terms of programming—activities are planned for twenty-six out of the thirty-day program, leaving not much room for extracurricula activities and free time. Especially, considering that alongside the planned visits to sites, students participate in structured debrief and reflection sessions and are tasked with completing assignments while traveling (those consist of eight classic research and reflection papers, fulfilling the eight credit requirements). "Difficult" in terms of both the emotional and physical demands placed onto the students. Many students voiced in their evaluation of the program that "*the responsibility felt about the Holocaust and knowledge about it caused stress.*" This often extended beyond the program, with an emotional impact felt "*when interacting with others back home.*"

Furthermore, there are the pedagogical/academic issues. For instance, the broader questions regarding the impact and purpose of on-site education that were introduced at the beginning of this chapter. That a significant impact exists, is of course undisputed and some examples have been given. However, opinions split as to the exact nature of the impact that these visits produce, and how such impact can be translated, compartmentalized, or measured. Some studies insist that there is indeed evidence that "being there," or, what Cowan and Maitles describe as "seeing inhumanity close up," in the context of programs such as student visits to Auschwitz, can achieve something very concrete in the personal development of students. The authors point to data that suggests, for instance, very specific cognitive/reflective influences such as an enhancement of students' citizenship values upon return [16] Others, however, insist that while *an* impact on the learner cannot be questioned, research in this area is speculative at best; as Carol Clyde writes in her examination of the impact of another experiential learning program—the March of Remembrance and Hope in which participants traveled to cities and historical sites in Poland—while an impact on the learners was anticipated, "it was uncertain what specific areas would be influenced." [17]

Much of the varying research findings point to a larger, and more essential, uncertainty as to the nature of knowledge produced; here, the core tensions emerge from the promise of *analytical* knowledge and *affective* one; as Hirsch and Kacandes suggest, "the greatest challenges for the teacher is enabling students to be self-conscious about their subject positions and their acts of co-witnessing, another is the disturbing tension between affect and analysis."[18] It should be clear that visiting sites and "being there" comes with particular demands that have to do with historical trauma: demands of witnessing, of bearing witness (support and endure), demands of forgetting and remembering (often simultaneously).[19] Many, if not most, of the sites we visit bear direct witness to the crimes of National Socialism, the consequences of anti-Semitism, the reducing of human beings to bare life, and subsequently, the horrors of mass killings. Research continues to show the strong emotional effect that visits to former sites of crime have on both teachers and students.[20]

Lastly, there are ethical issues that have their roots in two realms: To begin with, studies on the emotional impact on Holocaust education at sites of trauma ought to raise serious ethical concerns for educators (the focus of Chap. 4).[21] Attributes used by my students to describe their impressions upon visiting Sachsenhausen included *"heart-wrenching," "claustrophobic,"* and *"horror."* The other realm has to do with what has been captured as an ethical tension in the debate on "dark or death tourism" and have to do with the ways our gaze and spectatorship is deployed when looking at sites and images of suffering. Elizabeth Dauphinee offers an apt exploration of this tension, and here with an eye on the use of atrocity images, when she argues that the alleged

> 'ethical' use of the imagery of torture and other atrocities is always in a state of absolute tension: the bodies in the photographs are still exposed to our gaze in ways that render them abject, nameless, and humiliated—even when our goal in the use of that imagery is to oppose their condition.[22]

Students on this program are encouraged to reflect on their own role and obligations beyond the gaze when at sites of trauma, and to observe how, if at all, this may affect their learning experience. As one student observes while at the former Nazi Rally Grounds in Nuremberg:

> It struck me as strange that people were sitting on the slabs of stone that former concentration camp prisoners had made and these people seemed to have no idea where they were. They were laughing, drinking beer, or taking pictures seemingly without taking into consideration that thousands of Nazis had rallied there 70 years before

Together, my collection of encounters gestures toward a set of attributes to consider when navigating through these categories of issues on a journey with students at sites of trauma and violence. These attributes are by no means exhausted here, nor can they be. They certainly are anchored in something that James Young described as "received history": the "combined study of both *what* happened and *how* it is passed down to us." The writings here are a modest attempt to capture the effects of the past on the present; an enduring commitment to "true learning," to notions of inheritance of knowledge and history, and to thinking critically about the conditions we as educators provide.[23]

A NOTE ON METHODOLOGY: NARRATING STUDENT ENCOUNTERS

The methodology adopted here is ethnographic in nature and focuses on observing my group of students in their interaction at sites of trauma and violence in three consecutive years (2013, 2014, and 2015). I do not claim for this kind of ethnography to draw from the one used in an anthropological context that focuses strongly on an immersion within a group or society. While I was of course closely embedded with my students, my observations are not limited to my "objective" observations of them. What this means is that this book is narrated predominantly through the lens of encounters that registered with *me*, and that made an impact on *my* approach to Holocaust education that I had not previously considered. Moments that unsettled me, therefore, and often left me with notions of being "dispossessed": uprooted from my own assumptions and certainties about education, challenged about my presumed knowledge, and confronted with emotions and sensations I generally would not grant myself to experience as an educator (such as guilt or shame). Perhaps better understood therefore as a "critical ethnography," it gestures to a particular mindset of the educator.[24] This mindset has a particular goal; often, as in this case an ethical preoccupation. This ethnographic framework brings forth *my own* thoughts, ideas, and connections.

In this sense, the writings here—just as "all scholarly debates," argue Brigg and Bleiker— can be seen as "a type of storytelling."[25] This kind of autoethnographic approach is a means for setting an occasion that allows us to think through our strategies and tactics of teaching at sites of trauma. By doing so in terms of specific events, visits, and a particular program, this book stays away from broad generalizations on Holocaust pedagogy; instead, it offers a very focused, unique, and narrative-based insight into the currency of Holocaust teaching for educators, students, and practitioners in the discipline.

There are two main questions that structure the writings here; first, the one that asks to what extent we can bring the often-traumatic experiences of visiting sites of trauma and violence into the fold of learning about the history of those very sites. Here, related questions ask to what purpose we do indeed learn about the Holocaust to begin with, and what one ostensibly learns when visiting sites where mass killings took place.

Second, the one that investigates the extent to which there is a conflict between the ethical imperative to teach about the Holocaust—in order to remember such catastrophic past—and the impetus to find ways to teach about it "most effectively."

An additional set of, salient, questions aid to ground my observations. These questions were openly discussed with the student at various points during the program, and inform many of my observations here. The questions include the following ones:

What is the main motivation for participating in this study abroad program? What is the main motivation for studying the Holocaust? These questions are being asked as part of the official application procedure for which applicants have to write a narrative essay. It helps to gauge their academic background in the areas of study but also aids in evaluating their maturity and personal background.

How is the method of "being there" perceived and assessed? This question is discussed not only prior to departure—akin to the notion of "what do you wish to *see*"—but also throughout the program as part of the regular debrief sessions. Students are encouraged to discuss the benefits, and also limits, of what they have seen/experienced/and noticed during visits of sites. For instance, students often think through the impact that they themselves have on sites through their performances, and how it may impact on their experience—*"is it ok to have lunch at Auschwitz?"* This includes a reflection on *how participants perceive themselves at the sites (Tourists? Visitors? Students?). How does this perception inform the learning experience?*

How much are participants aware of the traumatic effects of their learning experiences? Students are encouraged to critically assess their own, emotional well-being during the course of the program. This is done in personal conversations but also within the debrief sessions within the larger group.

What can be described as the most valuable "take-away" from having participated in this program? This question yields at students' final evaluation of their journey, which is predominantly discussed upon return to the USA.

These questions are investigated mainly through my field notes, personal reflections on my role as the educator leading this program, and through student comments over the course of three years. Many of the students have worked closely with me on formulating these questions and in recognizing their importance for them and the program.

While these encounters are deeply personal they are clearly described here within the domain of Holocaust studies and pedagogy; they are theoretical in that they speak to some essential concepts of learning and teaching but are geared to demonstrate that these essential concepts are embedded in our—educators and students—life and experiences. By so doing, this study promises to achieve a set of important insights: By retelling my students' experiences through the lens of key encounters, I hope to illustrate how, and to what extent, the narratives and promises of Holocaust education seep into the lives of my students.

CHAPTER OUTLINE

There ought to be no doubt—and conversations with my students confirm this—that programs such as the one I have led can be described as stimulating, unique, and formative.[26] Students insist that *"I could read every piece of literature on the Holocaust and still not have the comprehensive understanding that I have gained from this trip,"* and, *"I will remember these days [of the program] for the rest of my life."*

Perhaps, and in line with the opening paragraph of this chapter, one should not find this surprising at all. But when contemplating less the assumed learning impact of "being there" and more other, perhaps salient, motivations for "seeing" representations of atrocity close up, important debates on the touristic explorations at sites of trauma must be confronted. After all, the allure of the gaze (the witnessing) and the presumed seductiveness of "seeing is believing," (the truth finding) are a well-documented phenomenon. It is often criticized in the literature through the concept of "trauma tourism" or "dark tourism," pointing to the limits of an ethical practice of witnessing the past—the modes of which are discussed in detail in the subsequent Chap. 2. It will become clear that a careful consideration of teaching at sites of trauma must necessarily begin with unpacking the complexity of historical trauma that *commands* our attention and remembrance, but simultaneously *demands* our resistance to other responses such as "mimicry, voyeurism, and spectatorship."[27]

Many of the encounters with my cohorts at sites of trauma had implications on my teaching about the Holocaust that I had not considered. In Chap. 5 specifically, I wrestle with the phenomenon that the Holocaust study abroad program has affected students in ways that I had not expected, and that I certainly was not prepared for. Students share how they are having dreams about their visits to sites, how they feel anxious about those visits, and how it affects their prior state of emotional health. This "secondary witnessing"—or experiencing the trauma of others through "being there"—is trauma nonetheless as students participate in the reexperiencing of the event.[28] Many of my observations confirm the emotional complexity of witnessing the memory of atrocity.

In Chap. 3, I explore the role of atrocity footage in general, and at sites in particular. Visual representations of the Holocaust are an integral of teaching at sites and I do not assert that there is no value in looking at atrocity imagery. However, using images (in the classroom and also at sites and museums) is a highly contested means by which to learn and teach about atrocities.[29] Grounded in studies coming out of the concept of "compulsory viewing," I take furthermore cues from Rebecca Adelman's study on Abu Ghraib images in teaching to make explicit the risks and ethical considerations of showing and using images of atrocity.[30]

Chapter 4 is interested in exploring that which is absent in the representations of the Holocaust. Visits to Ravensbrück Women's camp speaks to this notion of absence, or void, for my cohort in two ways: One has to do with the absence of visible traces of violence; here, I will explore the aesthetics of absence as a tool for teaching about the Holocaust—empty camp grounds, lack of visible structures, lack of visual representations. One important discussion here has to do with the question how absence of visible trauma affects learning. The other, and related to the concept of absence, is an exploration of the ways in which Ravensbrück is symbolic for the disappearing of discussions on the role of perpetrators in the memorial landscapes.

Chapter 5 asks if such experience is indeed necessary; in other words, to think through to what extent do we need to value experiencing trauma as a component of teaching about trauma. What follows is if we as educators can facilitate effectively a traumatizing experience, and how we may need to respond to the ethical and political implications of traumatizing students. These questions have roots in two thoughts: on the one hand, there is perhaps a fundamental impasse with regard to students' exposure to trauma when at sites of mass killing. That is to say, it is unavoidable and inevitable based on the consensus that the horror and shock of the Holocaust may *defy* assimilation into a comfortable framework for understanding and explanation. As Simon states, the Holocaust commands an attention "fraught with complex emotions."[31] On the other hand, and equally essential, is this question: if we command our students to "never forget" the Holocaust, does that mean they must have an unforgettable experience? Both of these roots suggest that pedagogy is closely intertwined with crisis and trauma when at sites of mass killing.

By way of concluding remarks, I will concede that this book is by no means to be understood as a comprehensive "road map" for how to conduct a Holocaust study abroad program-far from it. Nonetheless, the concluding chapter seeks to make some broader statements and suggestions that integrate ideas for future study abroad programs.

NOTES

1. Simon, R. and Eppert, C. (2005) 'Remembering obligation: witnessing testimonies of historical trauma', in Simon, R. (ed.) *The Touch of the Past. Remembrance, Learning and Ethics,* (Palgrave MacMillan), pp. 50–64.
2. Kranz, T. (2013) *The Pedagogy of Remembrance as a Form of Museum Education.* Clyde, C. (2010) 'Developing civic leaders through an experiential learning programme for Holocaust education', *Prospect,* 40, 289–306.
3. Dewey, J. (1938) *Experience and Education* (New York: MacMillan).
4. Trigg, D. (2009) 'The place of trauma: Memory, hauntings, and the temporality of ruins', *Memory Studies,* 2:1, 87–101.
5. Landsberg, A. (2004) *Prosthetic Memory: The Age of Transformation of American Remembrance in the Age of Mass Culture,* (Columbia University Press), p. 130.
6. Smith, S. (2007) 'Teaching about the Holocaust in the setting of museums and memorials', in Goldenberg, M. and Millen, R. (Eds.) *Testimony, Tension, and Tikkun,* (University of Washington Press), pp. 271–283.
7. Smith, 'Teaching about the Holocaust in the setting of museums and memorials'.
8. This framework is deeply influenced by the work of Elizabeth Dauphinee's writings on the ethics of research and scholarship. Dauphinee, E. (2010) 'The ethics of autoethnography', *Review of International Studies,*

36, 799–818; Dauphinee, E. (2007) *The Ethics of Researching War. Looking for Bosnia* (Oxford University Press).

9. Simon, R. and Eppert, C. (2005) 'Remembering obligation: witnessing testimonies of historical trauma', in Simon, R. *The touch of the past. Remembrance, Learning, and Ethics and Ethics* (Palgrave Macmillan), pp. 50–64.

10. Simon, *The touch of the past. Remembrance, Learning, and Ethics and Ethics*, p. 5.

11. Simon, *The touch of the past. Remembrance, Learning, and Ethics and Ethics*, p. 5.

12. Young, J. (1993) *The texture of memory*, (Yale University Press).

13. Brown, M. and Davies, I. (1998) 'The Holocaust and Education for Citizenship: the teaching of history, religion and human rights in England', *Educational Review*, 50:1, 75–83. Gray, M. (2014) *Contemporary Debates in Holocaust Education*, (Palgrave Pivot).

14. Blum, L. (2004) 'The Poles, the Jews and the holocaust: reflections on an AME trip to Auschwitz', *Journal of Moral Education*, 33:2, 131–148. Cowan, P. and Maitles, H. (2010) 'We saw inhumanity close up', *Journal of Curriculum Studies*, 43:2, 163–184. Schechter, H. and Salomon, P. (2005) 'Does vicarious experience of suffering affect empathy for an adversary? The effects of Israelis' visits to Auschwitz on their empathy for Palestinians', *Journal of Peace Research*, 2:2, 125–138.

15. Gray, *Contemporary Debates in Holocaust Education*.

16. Cowan and Maitles, '*We saw inhumanity close up*'.

17. Clyde, C. (2010) 'Developing civic leaders through an experiential learning programme for Holocaust education', *Prospects*, 40, 289–306, p. 304.

18. Hirsch, M. and Kacandes, I. (2004) *Teaching the Representation of the Holocaust*, (New York: The Modern Language Association of America), p. 19.

19. Simon, *The touch of the past. Remembrance, Learning, and Ethics and Ethics*, p. 51.

20. The European Union Agency for Fundamental Rights (2011) *Excursion to the Past—Teaching for the Future: Handbook for Teachers* Available: http://fra.europa.eu/en/publication/2010/excursion-past-teaching-future-handbook-teachers Accessed 10 March 2014.

21. Cowan, and Maitles, 'We saw Inhumanity Close Up', p. 176.

22. Dauphinee, E. (2007) 'The politics of the body in pain: Reading the ethics of imagery', *Security Dialogue*, 38, 139–155, p. 145.

23. Young, J. (1997, 41)

24. Auchter, J. (2014) *The Politics of Haunting and Memory in International Relations* (Routledge), p. 34.

25. Brigg, M. and Blieker, R. (2010) 'Autoethnographic International Relations: exploring the self as a source of knowledge', *Review of International Studies*, 36, 779–798.

26. Romi, S., and Lev, M. (2007) 'Experiential learning of history through youth journeys to Poland: Israeli Jewish youth and the holocaust', *Research in Education*, 78, 88–102.

27. Simon and Eppert, *The touch of the past. Remembrance, Learning, and Ethics and Ethics*, p. 53.

28. Felman, S. (1991) 'In an era of testimony: Shoah', *Yale French Studies*, 79, 39–81.

29. Bathrick, D. (2004) 'Teaching visual culture and the Holocaust', in Hirsch and Kacandes *Teaching the Representation of the Holocaust*, pp. 286–300.

30. Adelman, R. (2014) 'Atrocity and Aporiae: Teaching the Abu Ghraib Images, Teaching Against Transparency', *Cultural Studies and Critical Methodologies*, 12:1, 29–39.

31. Simon, *The touch of the past. Remembrance, Learning, and Ethics and Ethics*, p. 51.

CHAPTER 2

"*I Was There!*": The Conjunction of Study Abroad and Dark Tourism

Abstract When contemplating the role and promise of a Holocaust study abroad program, it is worth pausing here to note that many would see our visits to concentration camps and other sites of death as ghoulish and morbid, and charge us with what is understood as "trauma or dark tourism"— the traveling to places connected to death and atrocity. The concept of dark tourism brings up a set of interesting questions: To what extent does the program intersect with, and even constitute, tourism to Holocaust sites? If so, (how) does it matter? How does our role as tourists affect us in our learning outcomes but also affect the sites we visit? Furthermore, to what extent is our objective to learn at sites of trauma ethical when considering the charge of trauma, or dark, tourism? Set amidst a growing body of literature that focuses on the theoretical issues surrounding dark tourism, my observations here offer an opportunity to think about how we can negotiate the tensions between our roles as learners, visitors, and tourists. While my encounters certainly incorporate the charges that the label of dark tourism places upon us, they do offer a departure from the typically negative valance to suggest instead that an intentional reflection by students on the ways in which trauma and memory is mediated through tourism can add a valuable, and positive, methodological tool to learning about the Holocaust.

Keywords Trauma tourism · Dark tourism · Ethics · Spectatorship Voyeurism

© The Author(s) 2018   17
N. Bormann, *The Ethics of Teaching at Sites of Violence and Trauma*,
DOI 10.1057/978-1-137-59445-7_2

"Dark Tourism has come of age," claims Hartmann, suggesting that traveling to, and experiencing, places associated with death and suffering is by no means a new phenomenon.[1] In fact, it is argued that people have long been seeking out visits to sites associated with death, mass atrocity, and disaster, and they are compelled to doing so based on what Seaton summarizes as fundamentally a "thanatopic tradition"—an innate contemplation of death.[2] There is more to it; dark attractions are categorized along a continuum of shades of darkness (sites *of* death are seen as considerably darker than sites *associated* with death), while visitors' motivations can be equally seen on a continuum (of intensity)—ranging from a desire to fulfill curiosity, empathy, identity, and horror.[3] Needless to say, from Foley and Lennon's coining of the term "dark tourism" in the 1990s and their much cited work on *Dark Tourism: The attraction of Death and Disaster* to Seaton's initiation of another term—*thana*tourism—a rich body of literature continues to debate the growth of tourists flocking to sites of death and atrocity, the "supply and demand" classification of such tourism, and also the question of the efficacy of the term "dark tourism" itself.[4]

Research in tourism and heritage studies suggests that sites associated with war probably constitute the "largest single category of tourist attractions in the world."[5] Within that, it is in particular sites and places connected to the Holocaust that receive attention as perhaps the most "popular" tourist destinations. As Stone puts it, representations of the Holocaust are the "epitome of dark tourism."[6] This is especially interesting when one considers that mass killing sites constitute an enormous—and one might even argue impossible—task for comprehension and interpretation for visitors; and yet, "visitation to concentration camps continues."[7] The record visitor numbers to the museum site at Auschwitz-Birkenau only seems to confirm this—2 million people in 2016 alone visited the former German Nazi death camp in Poland.[8] Affirming the emotive label of dark tourism, the more critical commentators were quick to describe the site as the world's most unlikely "tourist hot spot" that is "so popular, they are turning people away."[9]

But what exactly is considered "dark" about dark tourism remains "eclectic and theoretically fragile."[10] Is it the sites themselves that provide an association with the dark aspect of tourism, or the collective experiences that visitors have at sites of death? Are we experiencing a growth of a demand for dark experiences (the tourists), or are we in fact seeing an increase of the supply of "darkness" (the sites themselves)?

Speaking specifically about the demand side and the act of traveling to dark sites itself, Stone proposes:

'dark'...alludes to a sense of apparent disturbing practices and morbid products (and experiences) within the tourism domain...it is suggested that dark tourism may be referred to as the act of travel to sites associated with death, suffering and the seemingly macabre.[11]

This includes also an emphasis given to the consumption and commodification of darkness by visitors, which often includes the modalities and habits of tourists at sites and the purchasing of, in this case, dark experiences.[12]

As already mentioned, a variety of motives are given for seeking out and consuming dark tourism; mostly, the literature suggests that being drawn to sites of death and suffering may have to do with our desire to see and experience something taboo—a human curiosity of mortality perhaps.[13] Ashworth is quoted as saying, "there are no dark sites, only dark tourists."[14] While some studies on Holocaust tourism insist that visits to the hundreds of memorial and museums in Central and Eastern Europe at authentic sites are driven by visitors' desire to honor the victims of the Nazi regime, or by a form of "educational tourism," others are quick to emphasize our prime interest in darker aspects of humanity.[15]

In an attempt to give greater clarification to the seeming demand for darkness, and to what Kansteiner described as our attraction to what we find "disturbing, fascinating, and intellectually challenging,"[16] there are suggestions that see the root of our seeking of darkness in the lack of visibility of death and suffering in the public realm in Western societies today—a phenomenon that Stone describes as the emergence of a thanatological condition in contemporary societies.[17] More specifically, and here borrowing from a term in sociological discourse, visitors are driven by a "purchasing of ontological security."[18] The term suggests that—in our daily lives—we are embedded in carefully maintained experiences of safety and a sense of order achieved "through various institutions and experiences that protect an individual from direct contact with madness, criminality, sexuality, nature and death."[19] Against that backdrop, dark sites are deviations from such ontological security, providing a means by which individuals may come into contact with what is undesirable in a controlled and benign environment. In other words, dark sites are an "opportunity" through which to experience death, which is increasingly concealed within Western society (Stone and Sharpley observe that "death becomes removed, abstracted, intellectualized, and depersonalized").[20] Dark tourist sites focused on death, "provide a means by which tourists can be allowed to indulge in their curiosity and fascination with thanatological concerns in a socially acceptable and, indeed, often sanctioned environment, thus providing them with an opportunity to construct their own contemplation of mortality."[21]

Furthermore, and here returning to sites that are less "of" death but "related to" a history of death, there are ethical charges leveled against wanting to simply satisfy our curiosities about famous sites[22]: A dark tourist, according to those studies, is drawn to the *recreational* attraction to places at which we *consume* atrocity experiences.[23] An example used often here is Hitler's former mountain retreat on the Obersalzberg—the "Eagle's Nest." While not an authentic site in the context used here—it was a site devoid of violence—visitors are attracted to experiencing how "it utterly chills to realize that the dark, mossy, overgrown ruins embedded in the landscape are remnants of the places where Hitler vacationed, entertained world dignitaries, and held meetings of strategic and military importance."[24]

Lastly, the dark tourism paradigm exposes and problematizes the modalities of what we do and how we act/react at sites—*how* we consume the experiences at sites. To put differently, the focus lies specifically on the performances as tourists, less on the sites themselves. What does the performance as a tourist entail, and how does this matter? One can think about altering existing spaces as we move through them in large groups, taking snapshots—I was there!—the way we dress. It also is important to think about the ways in which ("primary") visits to memorial and museum sites is couched in between "secondary" activities; for instance, holiday package deals offer a morning visit to Auschwitz and an afternoon trip to Poland's famous salt mines.[25] Much of this culminated in Cole's criticism of the commercialization and commodification of what is since then often denoted as "Auschwitz-land."[26]

Taken together, what these investigations into dark tourism illustrate—whether in form of thanatourism, grief tourism, ghettourism, or traumascapes—is that both in its consumption but also in its production it creates a significant amount of moral commentary.[27] What should be clear is that it is essential for those of us who visit these sites to take note of "the ethical obligations of all stakeholders," including learners as visitors.[28]

NEGOTIATING SHADES OF DARKNESS

Against the backdrop of charges that these various perspectives present, what are the educational challenges in conjunction with dark tourism? Especially when considering that the consumption of dark sites is not always intended, and the motivation is not necessarily a fascination with death or a curiosity with morbidity. Of course, capturing my students' motivations for participating in this study abroad program and with an eye on their rationale for visiting sites of death is fraught with difficulty in any reliable empirical format. As is discussed in Chap. 1, students claim to be compelled to sign on to the program for educational reasons, driven by a fascination with the history at sites, and often for personal reasons of identity and heritage. "*We have the right intentions,*" insists one student in response to our conversation about tourism. Here, I want to narrate some of our collective experiences at the sites, illustrate how students process the meaning of dark sites, before making suggestions on how to integrate the theoretical underpinnings of dark tourism into ideas for an educational framework for teaching at sites of death and trauma.

Each year, my students make purchases at the various camps' museum gift stores (whether it is at Dachau or at Auschwitz or elsewhere). While we stand in line to enter the memorial and museum sites, and as we wait for our guide to meet and greet us, some of us wander off into the conveniently located shop— usually adjacent to the site entrance. There, we can buy books and accompany study guides but also jewelry, key chains, fridge magnets, and postcards. Unsurprisingly, the availability of gift shops prompts some perplexed looks on my students' faces, and I am reminded of the tenor in Tim Cole's indicting book *Selling the Holocaust: From Auschwitz to Schindler how history is bought, packaged, and sold.*[29] As if in anticipation of such indictment regarding the availability of souvenirs and acts of consumerism at a former site of suffering, some stores are at pain to make it known that the revenues are being funneled back into the upkeep of the memorial sites—there is no profit to be made here.

There is something inherently uncomfortable though in the supply side of dark tourism and how we are invited to engage with it. Especially, because it points to something that is essentially difficult to reconcile: a practice that has to do with constructing a space of personal consumption and public attraction —of being a tourist with purchase—only a few feet and moments away from witnessing an often disturbing history of violence and death. One of my students buys a bracelet at the Dachau gift store—there is a small jewelery section on display—which she found especially beautiful. Perhaps, the student will wear it herself as a reminder of the relevance of the place where she bought it (though this would assume that the experience of visiting a former concentration camp needs a reminder against forgetting). Or perhaps the student will gift it, as a souvenir, for someone she cares about. I always wonder how the conversations may unfold when sharing those kinds of gifts: "I bought this for you at a concentration camp in Germany / Isn't it pretty / I love you."

We bring packed lunches for Dachau, which we eat while sitting on the lush and well-kept camp greens; we could easily be mistaken for having a picnic, carefully unwrapping sandwiches, and sharing snacks while taking a break in the sun. The days at camps are long and the café at the camp entrance can get quite busy with school groups and visitors. There is something about waiting in line for lunch at a former camp site that convinces us that bringing our own food that day is somehow morally superior, less touristy. On other occasions, however, we succumb and decide to eat at the conveniently located restaurant at the entrance of the museum at Auschwitz; "*the prices there are reasonable*," I hear someone utter. There is ice cream. We sit together around the restaurant table, desserts in front of us, and conversations quickly move from our experiences at the museum site to discussions about our dinner plans upon return to our hotel.

All of this can be shared with friends and family back home—after all, there is a post office for your postcards at Auschwitz and a money exchange office to make those purchases, too. Although, let us be honest, who still writes postcards? Instead, a spontaneous snapshot—a selfie even—and a quick upload onto one of our many social media outlets— "*is there wifi at Auschwitz?*"—will do just as well. "Wish you were here!" the tagline might read.

None of these encounters should come as news. They should neither come as a surprise, since some of these practices (see "selfies at Auschwitz") have been discussed publically and widely in mainstream media.[30] Nor is this meant to be self-righteous; far from it. In preparing and leading my students, I do *not* provide pre-given guidelines on how to act, behave, or think of sites of trauma: I refrain from warnings and suggestions; I do *not* ask them not to eat, or *not* to make purchases, and I do *not* prohibit taking photographs, or the use of cell phones. In fact, I would have *not* discouraged or judged my students if they had made use of the mist sprinklers at the entrance to the Auschwitz memorial museum site that was put in place to help visitors cool down and be more comfortable while touring the site during a very hot Polish summer. Needless to say, these showerheads were, too, at the center of a heated controversy about how much memorial sites should cater to the comfort of tourists.[31]

The students in the group often lament the conflict they feel regarding their identity as tourists and how to negotiate being a tourist with being a learner and the responsibility felt of becoming witness to past trauma. It is something they often condemn as inescapable—a role forced upon them due to the overall structure of the sites as tourist destinations to begin with. Yes, my students make purchases and eat lunch—because *they can.* "*I felt guilty sometimes,*" concedes one student; "*angry*" about tourists, says another. At the same time, students take note of sites as attractions by observing that "*seeing others react showed me how big the events actually were,*" and recognize the impact they have upon those structures. Thus, while we are funneled into the tourist trap—there are restaurants and shops—we also are aware of producing and altering the sites we visit—we *want* food and *ask* for memories to take home.

Incorporating Dark Sites into Study Abroad

The way people visit concentration camps reminds me of people going to the circus or stopping in traffic to watch a bad car accident despite knowing that it's wrong.

No doubt, the conjunction of tourism and learning at sites of trauma and violence can quickly descend into an ethical condemnation of students as purchasers of history, and of sites as "accommodating leisure markets."[32] Through the encounters with my students at sites, I want to depart from these stifling condemnations of trauma tourism. Instead, while my observations incorporate the fact that tourism and study abroad are perhaps inevitably bound up, they offer an alternative perspective on how to enhance tourist structures in ways that aid students in their learning experience.

"*Is it ok to eat at the camp site?*" is perhaps one of the most often asked questions during my experiences with students and in lieu of our visits to the camps. While I refuse to set guidelines for how to navigate the site structures—which would amount to a one-size-fits-all

approach to study abroad—we nonetheless find ways to reflect critically on questions of etiquette and appropriateness. It bears reminding that many of the sites give little indication for how to navigate
through the grounds. There are some recommendations with regard
to visitors' behavior (to act in ways that are deemed "respectfully" and
in accordance with the difficult emotional subject matter) but very few
direct rules are in fact given. There are "no smoking" signs outside
the former barracks at the Auschwitz site, or warnings to avoid step-
ping on foundations of former buildings—all that is sometimes left of
structures—that could easily be mistaken as an opportunity to sit and
rest on. But most sites stay away from being more specific than that. At
Auschwitz, for instance, during a conversation with a member of the
Press Office, we find out that "selfies at Auschwitz" are not denounced
or censored either.

What to wear, how to behave, what not to do or say, how to move
through the site? I suggest to students to make their own choices—such
as with regards to eating—but to make them mindfully and purposefully.
It is an invitation to think about why they would deem their behavior
as (in)appropriate, and how their actions may affect their—and others'—
experiences at the site. Why is it ok to bring lunch and eat where others
were once starved and killed? Through this thought process, they themselves establish a continuum of intensity of tourist sites and etiquette.
Often, students reflect on their own role as visitors to memorial sites in
relation to their observations of others and mutual observations of each
other in the group.

They notice, and fiercely lament, the group of teenagers, laughing
and goofing around seemingly ignorant of the fact that they are on the
grounds of a former camp; young adults busy on their phones, sharing messages and photographs ostensibly unperturbed by the fact that
they are engaging in these activities in the unnerving former examination room where prisoners at Sachsenhausen were enduring gruesome
medical experiments. There is a young teenage couple sharing a romantic
kiss on the Dachau camp ground that is the topic of conversation among
my students for some time to come—*"how can they?"*, *"how dare they?"*,
and *"they do not to care"*, sums up the main discussion points. *"There
were a few students taking pictures of themselves pretending to be killed
by the gas"*, reads one student's blog entry at the same camp. As Dekel
points out in her study of visitors' behavior at the Holocaust Memorial
to the Murdered Jews in Berlin, explorations of one's self in public and

at sites offer an important component of what she refers to as a transformative experience. These reflections are triggered by the landscape and scene provided by the site itself but also in regards to etiquette and "proper behavior" that we bring to the site.[33] For instance, a key aspect of visitors' experiences, according to Dekel, is exactly the observation of others—whether "playful, somber and touristy."

Students' observations of others become key talking points at the debrief sessions we hold regularly during our travels, and especially following days at former camp sites. I explain to my cohort that many of the teenage visitors they perceive as "behaving inappropriately" may likely be at the camp against their will; the education system in Germany has long debated, and has gone back and forth on, compulsory visits to concentration camps for middle and high school students.[34] It is very common for school groups to hold their history lessons at primary sites. This, in turn, opens up conversations about compulsory learning about the Holocaust in general—is there a responsibility to witness the trauma of the Holocaust, even against one's will? Is there a danger in forcing students to experience histories of violence and death?

In a related conversation, I instruct my students to think more empathetically about the giggling and seemingly careless teenagers at sites. I remind them that visits to sites of death and atrocity can be extremely traumatic for young adults (the age appropriateness for visits to a death camp such as Auschwitz is constantly discussed and revised amongst educators and experts).[35] The acting-out teenager who finds himself inside a former gas chamber or medical barrack where the most harrowing of experiments took place may not be intentionally careless or disrespectful at all—but it may just be his or her way of coping and dealing with a place that is simply too overwhelming to comprehend. This often leads into a deeper discussion on the role of vicarious trauma, the state of mind and health that we "bring" to sites, and I invite students to question the role of compulsory viewing of atrocity and shock as a pedagogical tool for learning about the Holocaust.

CONSUMERS OF DARK EXPERIENCES

There is no doubt—most dark tourism emphasizes the visual. Much of this has to do with the role that atrocity imagery plays in creating an affective encounter at the site—arguably, a reaction considered as central by dark sites as "suppliers" of an experience (I discuss this in detail in

Chap. 3). It is the result not only of arguments of the value of "shock" and notions of photographic evidence, but also of the many "habits" that visitors bring to the sites—including time constraints, limited attention spans, contemporary media influence, and expectations on visual literacy. My cohort often notices a *"fading of the emotional experience"* and feeling *"desensitized."*

The prevalence of visual evidence in the context of tourism lends itself to discussions on authorship and provenance of photographs. I remind my students that, more often than not, we are gazing at photographs produced by perpetrators—those behind the lens were Nazi officers who sought to capture images as trophies and propaganda material. This means, it was intended to be gazed at, to be seen, and to be circulated. This is not to suggest that we must not look at those photographs, but it allows us to think more carefully about what exactly we are gazing at, what this act of gazing means for us and our role, and what it means to document and share these images ourselves.

Some students insist that *"seeing is believing"* and that their photographs are evidence, or proof, of what they learned and saw, just as the photographs that they are looking at during our journey are evidence of past crimes. In our discussions, I counter this perception by questioning what these photographs, in fact, tell them? Here, we discuss the role of museums as representations of history, as perhaps staging and reconstructing history, and in assembling historical knowledge in particular ways. We always discuss at length the motivations for taking photographs at sites ourselves, especially since taking photographic evidence (see: I was here!) is one of the most recognizable tourist ritual. *"I took over 150 photographs,"* boasts one student. In our discussion, I encourage students to think carefully about why we feel compelled to visualize and memorialize through photographs.

Their tourist habit of photography—the taking of, staging, and posing for, photographs at sites prompts students to think more carefully about the role of memory, remembrance, and learning at sites. Most students say about their photography that they need images *"in order not to forget,"* which often leads to a very heated discussion on the assumption that—without an image—they would forget their experience at the site. Often, and this relates to the observations at the outset of this section, this has to do with a sense of feeling rushed during out visits and worries articulated by students that they may not have enough time *"to take it all in."* Here, photography becomes a crutch in their subsequent assembling of information; in other words, they feel compelled—if not forced—to take snapshot-like photographs due to the felt structural constraints. As we move further through the program, this perspective changes. For instance, an overnight stay adjacent to the site of Auschwitz-Birkenau and the longer time spent at the site relieves some of those concerns and students feel less coerced into the quick-shot memory ritual.

Related to the above arguments, we also discuss to what extent to engage in consuming dark tourism experiences by the purchase of photographs that we then circulate and share publically on social media. How different then is the iconic photograph taken at Auschwitz for public consumption from the souvenir bracelet bought at the Dachau camp store?

Lastly, some students take photographs for aesthetic reasons—to capture the gate, the barbed wire, and what they know to be iconic scenes. This provides a useful ground for discussions on iconic images and the ways in which Auschwitz represents the Holocaust to many of my students. How are these representations problematic?

Producers and Consumers of Dark Tourism

At the beginning of each programming cycle, still back on campus as I plan out the upcoming journey, I ask myself how many camp visits I need to include in this program. What message do I convey to my students by including as many camps as possible? Might this suggest that only by seeing and visiting former sites of death can we comprehend the history? Do I perhaps contribute to the production of dark tourism— adding to the demand side—by our visits? Each year, students' expectations culminate at our visit at Auschwitz where they then oscillate between notes that *"it gave me the result I was hoping for"* and *"where should we draw the line regarding the tourists."* Our sense of an identity as visitors is compounded by the fact that the sites we visit have multitude purposes. In other words, many of the tensions may emerge, partially at least, from the extent to which it is not always clear what kind of "destinations" these sites in fact are. Wollaston writes that most Holocaust museums are "simultaneously tourist attractions and memorial sites."[36] This adds an additional layer of complication to the roles that most former sites see themselves fulfilling —that of a museum (historical representation), a memorial (commemorative/pilgrimage function), and an educational institution (a *Mahnmal*, a "warning").

Back to Wollaston who adds that while it may be possible to distinguish between memorial and museum, the distinction "often becomes blurred."[37] What in fact *are* the students expected to encounter, experience, and take away from these three realms? And do they happen all at the same time? The danger may well be that these three roles are in conflict with one another.

In his provocatively titled book *Selling the Holocaust,* Cole spells it out for us: "Auschwitz is to the Holocaust what Graceland is to Elvis."[38] It is part of a larger critique of what he terms the "Holocaust Heritage Industry,"[39] and of museums as "marketplaces"[40] with experiences on offer we can purchase and consume. Many sites, such as Auschwitz, have a movie theater, a bookshop, cafeteria, restaurant, post office. There are long lines, perhaps even a security screening at the entrance just as we are used to when at the airport on our way to an exotic holiday destination. How can one not be made to feel like a tourist?

Ultimately, students conclude that the conjunction with the concept of trauma tourism "*does not diminish the learning component*" for them. When asked during an exit interview, back on campus, if study abroad always also means to be a dark tourist, students noted that they saw their role as tourists change in the course of the program: "*I felt less guilty toward the end when I became aware of my knowledge about the issue,*" suggested one student. Rather than denying the role of dark tourism within the context of this program, I argue that teasing out the specific features of the concept of dark tourism aids students in processing meanings, motivations, and learning outcomes.

NOTES

1. Hartmann, R. (2014) 'Dark tourism, thanatourism, and dissonance in heritage tourism management: new directions in contemporary tourism research, *Journal of Heritage Journalism* 9: 2, 166–182, p. 174.
2. Seaton, A. (2009) 'Purposeful Otherness: Approaches to the management of thanatourism', in Sharpley, R. and Stone, P. (Eds.) *The Darker Side of Travel,* (Bristol: Channel View Publications), pp. 75–108.
3. Golanska, D. (2015) 'Affective spaces, sensuous engagements: in quest of a synaestethic approach to 'dark memorials', *International Journal of Heritage Studies* 21 (8): 773–790. Ashworth, G. (2004) 'Tourism and the heritage of atrocity: Managing the heritage of South African apartheid for entertainment', in Singh, T. V. (Ed.) *New horizons in tourism: Strange experiences and stranger practices* (Basingstoke: CABI), pp. 95–108.

4. Lennon, J., and Foley, M. (2000) *Dark tourism: The attraction of death and disaster* (New York, NY: Continuum). Seaton, A. V. (1996) 'Guided by the dark: From thanatopsis to thanatourism', *International Journal of Heritage Studies* 2: 4, pp. 234–244. Foley, M. and Lennon, J. (1997) 'Dark Tourism - An Ethical Dilemma', in Foley, M. Lennon, J. and Maxwell, G. (Eds.) *Strategic Issues for the Hospitality, Tourism and Leisure Industries*, (London: Cassell), pp. 153–164. Sion, B. (Ed.) (2014) *Death Tourism: Disaster Sites as Recreational Landscape* (London; New York; Calcutta: Seagull Books).

5. Smith, V. (1998) 'War and Tourism: An American Ethnography', *Annals of Tourism Research*, 25, 202–227, p. 205.

6. Stone, P. (2009) '*The Darker Side of Travel*' (Channel View Publications), p. 58.

7. Lennon and Foley, *Dark tourism: The attraction of death and disaster*, p. 27.

8. Auschwitz-Birkenau Museum News (2017) 'Over 2 million visitors at the Auschwitz Memorial in 2016' Available http://auschwitz.org/en/museum/news/over-2-million-visitors-at-the-auschwitz-memorial-in-2016,1232.html. Accessed 1 March 2017.

9. Payne, E. (2015) 'Auschwitz becomes the world's most unlikely tourist hot spot', *Daily Mail UK Online* Available http://www.dailymail.co.uk/travel/travel_news/article-3052542/So-popular-turning-people-away-Auschwitz-world-s-unlikely-tourist-hot-spot-40-increase-visitors.html. Accessed 1 March 2017.

10. Stone, P. and Sharpley, R. (2008) 'Consuming dark tourism: A thanato-logical perspective', *Annals of Tourism Research*, 35. 2, 574–595, p. 575.

11. Stone, P. (2006) 'A Dark Tourism Spectrum: Towards a Typology of Death and Macabre Related Tourist Sites, Attractions and Exhibitions', *Tourism*, 54: 2, 145–160, p. 146.

12. Lennon and Foley, *Dark tourism: The attraction of death and disaster*.

13. Sharply, R. (2009) 'Shedding Light on Dark Tourism', in Sharply and Stone, *The Darker Side of Travel*, pp. 3–22.

14. Hartmann, 'Dark tourism, thanatourism, and dissonance in heritage tourism management: new directions in contemporary tourism research', p. 171.

15. Stone and Sharpley, 'Consuming dark tourism'.

16. Kansteiner, W. (2014) 'Genocide memory, digital cultures, and the aesthetization of violence', *Memory Studies* 7: 4, 403–408, p. 403.

17. Stone and Sharpley, 'Consuming dark tourism'.

18. Stone and Sharpley, 'Consuming dark tourism', p. 582.

19. Stone and Sharpley, 'Consuming dark tourism', p. 581.

20. Stone and Sharpley, 'Consuming dark tourism', p. 584.

21. Stone and Sharpley, 'Consuming dark tourism', p. 587.

22. Hartmann, 'Dark tourism, thanatourism, and dissonance in heritage tourism management: new directions in contemporary tourism research'.
23. Sharpley, R. (2016) 'Death Tourism: Disaster Sites as Recreational Landscapes. Book Review', *Journal of Policy Research in Tourism, Leisure and Events*, 8: 3, pp. 342–344.
24. Kaplan, B. A. (2011) *Landscapes of Holocaust Postmemory* (New York and London: Routledge), p. 11.
25. Wollaston, I. (2005) 'Negotiating the marketplace: The role(s) of Holocaust museums today', *Journal of Modern Jewish Studies*, 4: 1, 63–80, p. 65.
26. Cole, T. (1999) *Selling the Holocaust—From Auschwitz to Schindler: How History is bought, packaged, and sold* (New York: Routledge).
27. Stone, P. (2009) 'Dark Tourism: Morality and New Moral Spaces' in Sharply and Stone, *The Darker Side of Travel*, pp. 56–74.
28. Sharpley, 'Death Tourism: Disaster Sites as Recreational Landscapes. Book Review', p. 342.
29. Cole, *Selling the Holocaust—From Auschwitz to Schindler: How History is bought, packaged, and sold*.
30. Margalit, R. (2014) 'Should Auschwitz be a site for selfies?', *The New Yorker* Available http://www.newyorker.com/culture/culture-desk/should-auschwitz-be-a-site-for-selfies. Accessed 1 July 2014.
31. Mazza, E. (2015) 'Auschwitz summer cooling 'showers' angers visitors', *The Huffington Post* Available http://www.huffingtonpost.com/entry/auschwitz-showers_us_55e55415e4b0aec9f3546077. Accessed 10 October 2015.
32. Foley, M. and McPherson, G. (2010) 'Museums as Leisure', *International Journal of Heritage Studies*, 6: 2, pp. 161–174.
33. Dekel, I. (2009) 'Ways of looking: Observation and transformation at the Holocaust Memorial, Berlin', *Memory Studies*, 2: 1, pp. 71–86.
34. Bönisch, J. (2010) 'Scheinheiliger Pflichtbesuch', *Süddeutsche Zeitung*, Available http://www.sueddeutsche.de/karriere/nationalsozialismus-in-der-schule-scheinheiliger-pflichtbesuch-1.359663. Accessed 10 May 2017.
35. See for instance the official recommendation by Dachau Museum and Memorial Site 'Is the memorial site appropriate for children', Available https://www.kz-gedenkstaette-dachau.de/frequently-asked-questionsfaq/items/is-the-memorial-site-appropriate-for-children-9.html. Accessed 3 March 2017.
36. Wollaston, 'Negotiating the marketplace: The role(s) of Holocaust museums today', p. 66.
37. Wollaston, 'Negotiating the marketplace: The role(s) of Holocaust museums today', p. 66.

38. Cole, *Selling the Holocaust—From Auschwitz to Schindler: How History is bought, packaged, and sold*, p. 98.
39. Cole, *Selling the Holocaust—From Auschwitz to Schindler: How History is bought, packaged, and sold*, p. 110.
40. Wollaston, 'Negotiating the marketplace: The role(s) of Holocaust museums today'.

CHAPTER 3

"*And Now You Are Going to See Something Shocking*": Atrocity Images in Holocaust Education

Abstract Graphic representations of the Holocaust are seen as an absolutely integral, but also a highly contested, means by which to teach, learn, and remember Nazi atrocities. There are the black-and-white photographs and films that emerged from the liberation of the camps in 1945; the piles of corpses, hair, and shoes, and close-up shots of starved and emaciated prisoners behind barbed wire. These visual documents of hurt, injury, and suffering deliver not only proof of the horrors of the Holocaust but also imprint on us, the spectator, the demand to "never forget." They play a pivotal role in the museum narratives at the former camp sites but pose significant and largely unexplored pedagogical questions. This chapter begins by charting some of methodological challenges in working with atrocity imagery and their effect on learners. Recognizing ultimately the limits of students' abilities to respond to atrocity imagery, I reference an encounter devoid of graphic violence as a suggestion for a more ethically astute way to learn at sites of trauma.

Keywords Atrocity footage · Shock · Ethical spectatorship
Visual efficacy

"When should we see the dead?" asks David Campbell in reaction to a photograph shown in *The Guardian* newspaper in 2011: The image that prompted his question is that of a Libyan rebel surveying a possible massacre site of at least fifty burned bodies. It is a difficult image to look at,

© The Author(s) 2018
N. Bormann, *The Ethics of Teaching at Sites of Violence and Trauma*,
DOI 10.1057/978-1-137-59445-7_3

to say the least, and one that we do not see all that often. In Campbell's words, it is quite an "unusually graphic portrayal of war dead."[1] While images may play an increasingly important role—some speak of a "pictorial turn" in global politics to suggest our growing reliance on visual documentation to depict events and actors[2]—the production and circulation of atrocity imagery of recent wars is in fact far and few in-between; coverage has been mostly "sanitized" (from a save distance, covered up, or camouflaged) and certainly does not reflect the scale and intensity of death and suffering that has been caused in places such as Libya and elsewhere. To put it bluntly, pictures of the dead are a minority and thus at odds with the violent impact of war.[3]

There are many, obvious, reasons for the absence of atrocity footage in contemporary coverage of war. In the context of *The Guardian* image, the adoption of an "economy of taste and decency" through which the media itself regulates the representation of death and atrocity is certainly one of them (the image was only shown in the newspaper's online version).[4] While we may intuitively rush to label the media as "blood thirsty," the press does in fact err on the side of caution and restrain when it comes to depictions of death.[5] The recognition that images pose "thorny methodological challenges" is another reason for the lack of relying on violently graphic material. Particularly "thorny" is perhaps the fact that images "work differently from words."[6] That is to say, images are nonverbal but they need to be assessed and narrated which makes them "malleable - the perfect repository for projections of all kinds."[7] This means for instance that something always "gets lost in their interpretation."[8] Adding to the nonverbal nature is the fact that images work through emotions. These, in turn, are personal and internal phenomena and the effect of these emotions on the viewer remains notoriously difficult to assess.

But Campbell quickly follows up with another, related, question: *Should* we see more of the consequences of war? Overall, he concedes, yes, we should. Returning to the haunting image in *The Guardian,* he asserts that "words wash over us" whereas a photograph functions to make us pause and think—even if the event it points to is "too hard to stomach."[9] Robert H. Jackson, the Chief Prosecutor for the USA at Nuremberg, famously turned to the use of atrocity footage during the trial against Nazi perpetrators and insisted that the images spoke for themselves and offered testimony "where speech fails."[10] While others would quickly caution here that images alone cannot—and must not—determine the event,[11] there is an undisputed acknowledgment about this: "There is something unique about images. They have a special status. They generate excitement and anxiety."[12]

METHODOLOGICAL CHALLENGES

I wrestle with both of Campbell's questions—the "when" and "should" of atrocity imagery—each time when confronting my students with the often very graphic documents of the atrocities of the Holocaust. There are three main reasons for my reservations toward images during this program, and they align seamlessly with Bleiker's summary of three areas of methodological challenges that come with the use of images in general[13]: The first one has to do with the production of the image itself. This involves a consideration of the context in which the image was produced, reproduced, and circulated to begin with. There are significant ethical consequences that follow from that consideration. Specifically, one must remember that unlike the scarcity of graphic representations of contemporary war that Campbell speaks of, images of Holocaust atrocities do abound. With more than two million photographs existing in public archives, the Holocaust is one of the most visually documented events in history.[14] Yet, the visual material that meets us during our journey tends to be the repetition of the same few images; usually those who have gained iconic status and function as symbolic representations of the Holocaust (those images are mentioned further on in this chapter). This "obsessive repetition" is "disturbing," according to Hirsch, and really ought to make those of us who teach and study the Holocaust pause for thought: Why, she probes, with so many images available has our visual gateway for understanding the Holocaust been so "radically delimited"?[15] Do we, as educators, participate in this delimitation?

The second challenge speaks to the content of the image itself. To me, this raises questions about the circumstance within which the images were taken and to what extent those portrayed relate to, and interact with, the content of the image. We know that most Holocaust photographs were taken by the perpetrators; with very few images taken by the victims. This inevitably raises questions on the politics and ethics entailed in the staging and publicizing a perpetrator-authored image. The Nazis were "masterfull" in recording their rise to power and in documenting the atrocities they committed, and many of the photographs we see were taken by former camp guards for the purpose of recording and displaying their efforts of destruction.[16] As Hirsch points out, some photographs "present victims who were shot by the camera not long before they were shot and killed."[17] These two actions cannot, and should not, be readily disjointed. Even more notable than the brutality of the act of killing that we can see in the images of piles of dead, starved, and hurt bodies is the fact that some of the photographs show the perpetrators themselves who carried out that crime, or groups of onlookers who attended the scenes. Thus, the impunity with which these act were documented shock us.[18] It also means, the images were not only taken against the will of the bodies that they display but they were displayed as prey and for spectators to be seen. And while those photographs may have become an important instrument for the proof of Nazi atrocities, we cannot be evacuated from the fact that we are gazing at a suffering and humiliated body. As Dauphinee reminds us, the circulation and contemporary use of the imagery cannot (and must not) be separated from the violent production of that image in the first place.[19] I wonder, is an ethical viewing possible in the context of this program?

The third challenge—the biggest obstacle, I argue—has to do with how the audience, here the learner, receives the image and its content. It bears reminding that amongst those multitude of Holocaust images are the kinds of portrayals that Campbell might refer to as "too hard to stomach": Meeting us head on during our program are the harrowing black-and-white photographs and films that emerged from the concentration and death camps in the Spring of 1945; images that Susan Sontag described as the "photographic inventory of ultimate horror"— for instance, the wagonload full of corpses at Dachau that the arriving soldiers were exposed to. These images yield a significant possibly for learners to become (re)traumatized. I side with Hirsch here when she cautions that the repeated images of the Holocaust "need to be read from within the discourse of trauma, not for what they reveal, but for how they reveal it."[20] What are the ethical implications of (re)traumatizing my students?

Taking all three challenges together, it is clear that there is a "certain messiness" inherent in the act of spectatorship itself.[21] I take cues from Adelman and Kozol and argue that it is imperative for educators to confront the practices of spectatorship and to establish an ethical orientation for students toward their gaze at suffering of others.[22] Much of the problematic aspect of spectatorship is anchored in our expectation toward images *to do something for us*; assumptions about the "power of the image" to compel us to be moved make us lazy in *our* responsibilities *toward* the image and the people depicted in it. However, it is questionable what exactly images provoke, evoke, and task us to do. Specifically, in the context of the study abroad program, this translates into asking in what ways atrocity images of the Holocaust facilitate or inhibit our understanding of it, and under the burden of our gaze?[23] We assume an instrumentalizing approach to imagery even though we do not know the effect that depictions of injury have on our students. We also risk engaging in objectifying the people in those images, "pressing them into political service, without their consent, apparently for their own good."[24] Looking to Dauphinee again helps to emphasize the responsibility that comes with relying on images to teach the abhorrence of the Holocaust; she critically observes, "the bodies in the photographs are still exposed to our gaze in ways that render them abject, nameless and humiliated—even when our goal in the use of that imagery is to oppose their condition."[25]

Considering these hints at the main methodological challenges and the questions they raise for me during the program, two encounters stand out in particular as memorable—one has to do with a sense that learning at sites of trauma comes with the, often unquestioned, imperative to make atrocity visible; the other has to do with an experience that resisted this very process.

RETHINKING THE EFFICACY OF ATROCITY IMAGERY

Just as in *The Guardian's* portrayal of the Libyan rebel discovering a massacre site of burned bodies, footage of the liberation of Nazi camps captures the moment as the Western Allies made their own ghastly discovery upon arrival at the gates of Buchenwald, Bergen-Belsen, and Dachau. In an attempt to somehow grasp the unimaginable atrocity that was presented right in front of them, and to narrate this discovery for which there were no words, the soldiers picked up their cameras and started filming. The camera became a means, if not the only means, of truth telling. Given their iconic status, most of us are familiar with those very images; Marianne Hirsch reminds us of their content:

Close-up shots of individuals show bodies and faces apparently stripped of everything that the Western imagination associates with meaningful human existence: individuality, personality, reason, dignity. Long shots show masses of bodies strewn, piled, stacked, or dumped on the earth – bodies converted into things, bodies that no longer had anything to do with persons[26]

What to do with these images in the context of teaching? After all, we encounter this footage frequently during our program; it plays a central role in the museum narratives at former sites of violence, such as Dachau, where these images are used to frame the narrative of Nazi atrocity and to bring home the reality of the crimes committed at those very sites. We, too, watch the liberation footage that Hirsch describes as part of our site visit at Dachau. The minimum age requirement is fourteen, reflective of the concern regarding the graphic nature of some of the images it includes.[27] Students often find the footage intolerable; as one of my students confesses during our program, "*to see actual footage of freezing, emaciated people was frankly scary.*"

Images work through emotions.[28] And so the consumption of these images in the context of teaching—often deemed as "so overwhelmingly horrific that teachers should show them with extreme caution, if at all"[29]—has been debated over the years.[30] This has to do with the visceral and strong emotional reactions to atrocity footage that learners may exhibit—"usually of shock and terror, of compassion as well as rejection."[31] There are some who insist that this relationship between spectatorship and the image is, in fact, an essential component of learning about the Holocaust; Andre Singer, who directed the documentary *Night Will Fall* that is based on the discovery of the original atrocity footage of Nazi camps, asserts "we can only truly understand the horror of war if we use images like this."[32] But how does "understanding horror" really translate into measurable and productive outcomes—what in fact do we learn by seeing atrocity?[33] And more broadly, "what do images 'do' and don't 'do.'"[34] The question what images can really tell and teach us is rooted in expectations that graphic portrayals of suffering, trauma, and violence *should* provoke viewers/students into action. Faith in the image's ability to do so is predicated, in turn, on the assumption that graphic depictions of atrocity will be intense enough to horrify viewers into responding. But it is often unclear what this action may be, and if it can in fact be determined or influenced. This is not new, and continues to unsettle scholars who quickly point to the more recent example of the horrific torture images that leaked out of Abu Ghraib. In light of the fact that these images where deemed "spectacular" and "somehow exceptional" (read: intense enough to horrify) we were faced with "the apparent conundrum that such shocking images have had so little public effect."[35]

But there are more layers to the possible stifling or traumatic effects on the learner's emotional health resulting from the gaze at often gruesome suffering.[36] What may complicate the receiving of shock and horror is that atrocity footage leaves the learner exposed in their inability to respond; images of suffering often leave us paralyzed and restrained in our agency.[37] Taken together, we would rather look away than look at. If we cannot engage in these questions fully, and if we cannot assume that reactions to atrocity imagery are translatable, we may merely become complicit in what Selzer calls a "wound culture"—a societal pathology that exhibits itself in its public fascination, if not fetishism, with shock and trauma (and something that I discuss in Chap. 2 on trauma tourism).[38] Sontag felt strongly about the shock value of atrocity footage though she was equally adamant about the loss of that value over time.[39] The argument of the power of photographs to provoke is countered often with the common view that the proliferation of those photographs creates "compassion fatigue" in us.[40] However, and as Campbell points out, compassion fatigue suggests, again, that the image can be solely held responsible for its effect. By so doing, the notion of fatigue glances over the fact that an images' power relies on the "networks of practices" through which it is restricted or enabled.[41] This may mean to think carefully about the particular title of the image, the framework within which it is shown, or the social context within which it is circulating.

An example of the ways in which the effect of atrocity imagery must not be seen in isolation but rather in the context of a set of practices is our visit to the Auschwitz memorial museum; specifically, the ways in which the images and items on display are narrated and underwritten by the museum guides. Student groups get the sense that the guides are at pains to make visible the suffering that is symbolized through the features in the museum. My students are irritated by the display of atrocity and the centrality thereof, which often seem out of place if not exaggerated for visitors' consumption. Our guide at the museum at Auschwitz appears to try (too?) hard to stage experiences of suffering for the group: "*Look at the shoes* [the piles of shoes of former prisoners on display at the museum]," he emphasizes, "*look at the size of the shoes* [pointing to the children's shoes – which of course we can all see without being pointed at]". He continues: "*but that's not all - now we are going to see something even worse."* The narration appears forced, if not utterly out of place. Traveling through the exhibit is akin to a game, a challenge: how long can learners gaze at the items behind the glass and listen to the gruesome narrative before moving to the next. I notice myself tightening up—I gaze at my students who, in turn, stare at the guide, eyes wide open. One student immediately asks me, anxiously, *"if we are going to have this guide for the whole day."* Yes, we are.

This is not an argument about the quality of guides at sites. But this is about the ways in which the setting of the museum within which the content of the photographs are embedded produces certain practices that act as caption for these images. When speaking to students during our debrief sessions upon their return to the USA, what is frequently cited as their most valuable take-away from studying at historic sites is the notion that it *"makes the horrors tangible."* But does it do so through the means of *seeing* atrocity? I am not so sure. In that same context, students also reveal what they deemed as the most *"emotionally daunting"* experience that brings home the horror of the Holocaust are often *not* the images of violence and death but those of life (they are referring here specifically to images depicting Jewish Life *before* the war in the Shoah exhibit—(Block 27). To put it differently, the idea of horror is made most tangible for them not by images of death and suffering but by that of the lives lost and suffered through.

But emotions are notoriously difficult to assess. It is difficult to isolate emotions and identify what a genuine emotional response is, or quantify and label them as they are deeply personal and subjective.[42] Jim Johnson adds his skepticism about affective spectatorship in those ways and argues that the idea of atrocity photographs causing an affective reaction is "wrongheaded to begin with."[43] By which he suggests that we may be wrong in assuming that being a site of provocation makes the image necessarily an instrument for change. Johnson's interjection, as I see it, raises two important questions: On the one hand, what does an emotional response, in fact, motivate one to do, or, what does it ostensibly lead to? To put it differently, are compassion or sadness even politically meaningful or ethically relevant in the context of studying the Holocaust? Back to Johnson who discards any real value of compassion in terms of political action, arguing that it is "inevitably ineffective."[44]

On the other hand, and perhaps more relevant for us as educators, how do we know that it is indeed compassion that is produced? Johnson points out the danger of other affective responses, including pity, cynicism, resentment.[45] The danger of these "other" emotional reactions is on the obvious: pity and sorrow do not motivate learners necessarily to act upon their feelings; in fact, it is most likely to create a distance between them and the other for whom they have these emotional responses. Can we as educators influence the ways in which certain emotional responses are triggered—but not others?

Arguments regarding the efficacy of circulating and seeing atrocity imagery are of course not new: Coined as "compulsory viewing," the German population was forced to gaze at the aforementioned atrocity footage that came out of the concentration camps immediately after the end of the war. This required viewing was rooted in the very assumption that "seeing" would ultimately produce a sense of collective shame, guilt, perhaps horror—all of which was said to manifest itself in a policy of prevention of a repeating of atrocity, and a countering of a denial of atrocity.[46] However, subsequent studies found that the effect of such exposure was ambiguous and inconclusive at best. Meaning, most of the "first" viewers of these images accepted them as documents of "facts and proof" but not the interpretation that meant to come along with it. Germans appear to say "we do not recognize ourselves [and emotions of guilt, and empathy] in these images."[47] To me, this shows that—above all—the significance of the social context for the creation of pictorial meaning is central in our consideration of showing atrocity imagery to learners. As Campbell argued, "the same pictures can mean different things at different times because of different concerns."[48] In other words, images alone are not responsible for the images' power and thus not responsible for the effect we seek to see in the learner.

WHAT IF WE CANNOT SEE? ALTERNATIVES TO ATROCITY IMAGES

I agree with both Campbell and Dauphinee that visual representations may have the capacity to animate important forms of political resistance.[49] And it is exactly that which makes the questioning of the use and ethics of imagery very difficult. The "power of the image" is a recurring theme when discussing Holocaust education. As such, the intent here was not to trivialize or dismiss the role that atrocity footage — images and narratives—play for the teaching the Holocaust. My thinking about the role and use of atrocity imagery was triggered by two questions Campbell asked—"when should we see the dead" and "should we see the dead." But along the way, there is of course a third question to be asked implicitly: "Why would we lament the disappearance of the dead" in visual documentation? My queries had to do with the affective responses in students to the graphic documentation of atrocity and with how images might matter if they do *not* compel the spectator to act, or, to act in certain ways. There is, however, another convincing argument to be made in support of a more mindful approach: images can make us blind.[50] In the context of the imagery discussed here, this can have two meanings. To become blind to seeing images can relate to Sontag's note about the fading effect of photographs that are iconic. She argues, "photographs shock insofar as they show something novel"; but once they are seen over and over again, a saturation point may be reached.[51] Images can anesthetize. I already pointed out that atrocity footage of the Holocaust is widely accessible and has been reprinted countless times, which may inevitably result in the very effect that Sontag predicts. In fact, some would add that we have long surpassed that moment of saturation. There is more to it, however; as iconic images, they have also become canonized and used as symbolic representation for atrocities at large and beyond the historical context in which they emerged: Frames of half dead, naked survivors; piles of corpses; open mass graves; starved prisoners standing behind barbed wire—they all have become prototypes through which we refer to, access, and remember the inescapable dimension of contemporary atrocities. As Brink recounts, the images of emaciated men behind barbed wire in prison camps in the former Yugoslavia striking resemble those of 1945. The bulldozers that are photographed scooping up piles of corpses into mass graves in Rwanda look like Bergen-Belsen.[52] Atrocities "never stay in the past."[53] Rather, they are continuously witnessed and translated through their visual framing.

But images also make us blind in another way. Atrocity footage often isolates the moments of shock and terror, leaving behind the complexities of the event leading up to that moment captured in the image. Hannah Arendt convincingly remarked, "pictures of concentration camps are misleading insofar as they show the camps in their final stages." The imagery and sight of starving, half dead bodies by which we often associated the Holocaust with, Arendt explains, was in fact not typical at all for German camps—"extermination was handled by gas, not starvation." In other words, what we take to visually represent the Holocaust is, in fact, the aftermath thereof; when the image was taken the extermination equipment had already been dismantled, the visible starvation a result of the final months of a war.[54] To put it bluntly, in a "working" concentration camp there are no piles of corpses; the dead were cremated straight away.[55]

Therefore, and while the emotional experience of seeing atrocity imagery can be significant and staggering, during a five-week program I cannot help but notice that everyday seeing turns into such blindness amongst my students. I suggest that alternatives to the use of this kind of spectatorship exist, and do so in meaningful ways. And so, another way to perhaps query the role and promise of using images of atrocity is by thinking through encounters during this study abroad journey that were in fact *devoid* of visible atrocity imagery (see Chap. 4 on Ravensbrück). There is one encounter in the program that stand out in particular: The vast and empty landscape imagery at Auschwitz-Birkenau that acts as a symbolic space of "where once the gas chambers and ovens were." My students regularly refer to the area of Auschwitz-Birkenau as a landscape that conveys for them the *"real scale of the horror"* of the Holocaust. This sense of scale is brought to us visually—the vast landscapes—as well as through the experience of the time and effort it takes to see and absorb that landscape (by walking).

The experience of being able to "imagine" the extent of horror through images devoid of death is well articulated by Battani who speaks to the ways in which we connect with structures and compositions of landscapes—through what he describes as our "sociological imagina tion."[56] In short, imagination is necessary to any apprehension of suf- fering, especially if the circumstances of that suffering are so radically different and removed from our own.[57] Couched within the argument that our appreciation of atrocity footage is very much anthropocentric— seeing the dead *body*—is "unnecessarily narrow," the author purports that experiencing the vast and empty landscape of Birkenau may perhaps generate an emotional affect that runs counter to the one [atrocity foot- age] with which we have become all too familiar.[58] Battani explains: "it does not immediately shock and then become less shocking," rather, the opposite is at play here; first perhaps deemed as an empty and devoid space, an image such as Birkenau (or strolling across the lush landscapes of a former camp site) only becomes disturbing and challenging over time as we come to recognize our all-too easy embrace with the land- scape aesthetic as problematic. Students support that argument in their observation of the "*eeriness of the aesthetics of the green and lush land-scapes at Birkenau*" (but also Dachau); of "*leisurely walking through the grounds that are beautifully composed of trees and grass.*"

Battani reminds us that looking at human atrocity "close up," and being there, may counter-intuitively create distance as opposed to closeness. This is so exactly because it subverts "the bonds of human decency"—we are forced to stare and gaze at suffering which violates our social norms.[59] We feel immediately implicated in the crime, which is exacerbated by our continuous gaze; our return to the image again and again to make sense of it. He concludes: "we come to resent it" and such overwhelming emotional response is what renders a rational response "absurd."[60] The landscape devoid of the above, on the other hand, draws us in over a longer period of time—the longer I look, the deeper I look, the better I recognize the variety of connections between that very landscape and its dark past. Battani speaks here of the subversive power of the image and the demands it places upon us, the spectator/viewer—which is not compassion but structural thinking. Perhaps using another, more simple act/example may illustrate this better: Initially, students quite easily embraced the fact that they are repeatedly, and seemingly easily, walking in and out the gate of Auschwitz during our 2-day visit; this, however, changed after numerous of such moments and was deemed as "*disturbing*" and "*creating a sense of privilege that the prisoners did not have in that environment.*"

Perhaps less spectacular and gruesome presentations of violence, those that refuse to provide a disturbing jolt, might provide a different kind of engagement for students. In other words, becoming aware of participating in an—perhaps even "banal"—activity that was not available to those who suffered at the sites—walking in, walking out, enjoying the beautiful landscapes, eating at the camp site restaurant, stopping for a sip of water, using the restrooms as we please—also violates our social norms. But I would argue it does so in much more structural, impactful, and less paralyzing ways. As Adelman and Kozol point out that we should avoid focusing exclusively on *our* feelings when confronted with atrocity. Similarly, they argue, we must not focus exclusively on the other in those graphic documentations as it runs risk of objectifying and distancing the other who is depicted. The real meaningful experience may lie in the moment when we recognize the ties between the two in a "candid accounting of what is possible."[61]

NOTES

1. Campbell, D. (2011) 'Thinking Images v.21: Seeing the Dead'. Available: https://www.david-campbell.org/2 011/08/30/thinking-images-v-21-seeing-the dead/ Accessed 10 May 2013.
2. Bleiker, R. (2015) 'Pluralist Methods for Visual Global Politics', *Millennium*, 43:3, 872–890.
3. Bleiker, 'Pluralist Methods for Visual Global Politics'.
4. Campbell, D. (2004) 'Horrific blindness: Images of Death in Contemporary Media' *Journal for Cultural Research*, 8:1, 55–74.
5. Campbell, 'Thinking Images v.21: Seeing the Dead'.
6. Bleiker, 'Pluralist Methods for Visual Global Politics', p. 873.
7. Linfield, S. (2001) 'Beyond the Sorrow and the Pity', *Dissent* 48:1, 100–106, p. 104.
8. Bleiker, 'Pluralist Methods for Visual Global Politics', p. 873.
9. Campbell, 'Thinking Images v.21: Seeing the Dead'.
10. (in Douglas 1995, 452).
11. Sontag, S. (1977) *On Photography*, (London: Penguin Books).
12. Bleiker, 'Pluralist Methods for Visual Global Politics', p. 875.
13. Bleiker, 'Pluralist Methods for Visual Global Politics', p. 877–878.
14. Hirsch, M. (2001) 'Surviving Images: Holocaust Photographs and the Work of Postmemory', *The Yale Journal of Criticism*, 14:1, 5–37.
15. Hirsch, 'Surviving Images: Holocaust Photographs and the Work of Postmemory', p. 8.
16 Hirsch, 'Surviving Images: Holocaust Photographs and the Work of Postmemory', p. 7.
17. Prager, B. (2008) 'On the Liberation of Perpetrator Photographs in Holocaust Narratives', in Bathrick, D., Prager, B. and Richardson, M. (Eds.) *Visualizing the Holocaust*, (Rochester, New York: Camden House), pp. 19–37.
18. Campbell, 'Horrific Blindness'.
19. Dauphinee, E. (2007) 'The Politics of the Body in Pain: Reading the Ethics of Imagery', *Security Dialogue* 38:2, 139–155, p. 145.
20. Hirsch, 'Surviving Images: Holocaust Photographs and the Work of Postmemory', p. 12
21. Adelman, R. and Kozol, W. (2014) 'Discordant Affects: Ambivalence, Banality, and the Ethics of Spectatorship', *Theory & Event*, 17:3.
22. Adelman and Kozol, 'Discordant Affects: Ambivalence, Banality, and the Ethics of Spectatorship'.
23. Bathrick, D. (2004) 'Teaching visual culture and the Holocaust' in Hirsch, M. and Kacandes, I. (Eds.) *Teaching the Representation of the Holocaust* (New York: Modern Language Association of America), pp. 286–300.

24. Adelman and Kozol, 'Discordant Affects: Ambivalence, Banality, and the Ethics of Spectatorship'.
25. Dauphinee, 'The Politics of the Body in Pain: Reading the Ethics of Imagery', p. 145.
26. Hirsch, 'Surviving Images: Holocaust Photographs and the Work of Postmemory', p. 15.
27. KZ Gedenkstätte Dachau 'Notes on the Documentary film 'The Dachau Concentration Camp 1933–1945'. Available https://www.kz-gedenks-taette-dachau.de/documentary_film.html Accessed 1 May 2016.
28. Bleiker, 'Pluralist Methods for Visual Global Politics'.
29. Totten, S. (2002) *Holocaust Education: Issues and Approaches*, (Boston: Allyn and Bacon), p. 213.
30. Bathrick, 'Teaching visual culture and the Holocaust'.
31. Brink C. (2000) 'Secular Icons: Looking at Photographs from Nazi Concentration Camps', *History & Memory* 12:1, 135–150, p. 135.
32. Jeffries, S. (2015) 'The Holocaust Film that was too shocking to show', *The Guardian*. Available https://www.theguardian.com/film/2015/jan/09/holocaust-film-too-shocking-to-show-night-will-fall-alfred-hitch-cock Accessed 12 June 2015.
33. Bathrick, D., Prager, B. and Richardson, M., (Eds.) (2008) *Visualizing the Holocaust: Documents, Aesthetics, Memory* (Rochester, NY: Camden House).
34. Adelman and Kozol, 'Discordant Affects: Ambivalence, Banality, and the Ethics of Spectatorship'.
35. Adelman and Kozol, 'Discordant Affects: Ambivalence, Banality, and the Ethics of Spectatorship'.
36. Totten, S. and Feinberg, S. (2001) *Teaching and Studying the Holocaust* (Boston: Allyn and Bacon).
37. Adelman and Kozol, 'Discordant Affects: Ambivalence, Banality, and the Ethics of Spectatorship'.
38. Selzer, M. (1997) 'Wound Culture: Trauma in the Pathological Public Sphere', *October* 80: Spring, 3–26, p. 3.
39. Sontag *On Photography*, p. 21.
40. Campbell, 'Horrific Blindness'.
41. Campbell, 'Horrific Blindness'.
42. Bleiker, 'Pluralist Methods for Visual Global Politics'.
43. Battani, M. (2011) 'Atrocity Aesthetics: Beyond Bodies and Compassion', *Afterimage* 39: 1&2, 54–57, p. 2.
44. Battani, 'Atrocity Aesthetics: Beyond Bodies and Compassion', p. 2.
45. Battani, 'Atrocity Aesthetics: Beyond Bodies and Compassion', p. 2.
46. Carruthers, S. (2001) 'Compulsory Viewing: Concentration Camp Film and German Re-education' *Millennium* 30:3, 733–759.

47. (Brink, 66).
48. Campbell, 'Horrific Blindness', p. 71.
49. Dauphinee, 'The Politics of the Body in Pain'.
50. Brink, 'Secular Icons'.
51. Sontag, *On Photography*, p. 21.
52. Brink, 'Secular Icons', p. 136.
53. Lezra, E. (2014) 'A Pedagogy of Empathy for a World of Atrocity', *The Review of Education, Pedagogy and Cultural Studies* 36, 343–371, p. 346.
54. Brink, 'Secular Icons', p. 141.
55. Brink, 'Secular Icons'.
56. Battani, 'Atrocity Aesthetics: Beyond Bodies and Compassion', p. 57.
57. Adelman and Kozol, 'Discordant Affects: Ambivalence, Banality, and the Ethics of Spectatorship'.
58. Battani, 'Atrocity Aesthetics: Beyond Bodies and Compassion', p. 54.
59. Battani, 'Atrocity Aesthetics: Beyond Bodies and Compassion', p. 57.
60. Battani, 'Atrocity Aesthetics: Beyond Bodies and Compassion', p. 57.
61. Adelman and Kozol, 'Discordant Affects: Ambivalence, Banality, and the Ethics of Spectatorship'

"We Didn't Know There Was a Women's Camp": The Haunting Qualities of Ravensbrück

Abstract The question of absence and loss is central to invoking and representing the atrocities of the Holocaust. One only needs to think of the piles of shoes and other belongings at Holocaust memorial sites that powerfully evoke the absence of the people to whom these items once belonged. Illustrations of absence also register the destruction that those who once wore the shoes and owned the belongings had to endure and suffer through. To learn about, and experience, the Holocaust through this lens of absence can often be traumatic, if not frightening, for students. In this chapter I borrow from scholars who use the vocabulary of "ghostly" and "haunted" qualities in relation to our intricate encounter with Holocaust sites that evoke feelings of absence. The concept of haunting offers a valuable framework to make intelligible the affective responses that I register with my students at the women's camp Ravensbrück. What is distinctive about our encounter here is that the particular structure of the camp does not only gesture toward an intricate feeling of loss of lives, it also probes students to contemplate the fact that the narratives of female victims and perpetrators are also absent in the larger context of Holocaust teaching and learning.

Keywords Gendered experience · Ravensbrück · Aesthetics Memorial landscape · Haunted

© The Author(s) 2018
N. Bormann, *The Ethics of Teaching at Sites of Violence and Trauma*,
DOI 10.1057/978-1-137-59445-7_4

When we get off the train in a small town called *Fürstenberg*—about one hour north of Berlin—I admit to my group of students that I am not quite sure which way we are in fact going. This is my first time here, too: There are neither obvious signs for the *Gedenkstätte Ravensbrück* (the Memorial site Ravensbrück), nor is there the usual crowd of people that we have grown accustomed to already when approaching many of the Holocaust memorial sites and museums throughout our journey. Perhaps, our disorientation should come to no surprise; the camp location, set amidst forests and lakes, was chosen by Heinrich Himmler as a site far enough away for people not to know about it yet within reach of the train station we just arrived at.

From the train station, it is perhaps a thirty minutes walk through a sleepy town. The streets are empty; the sidewalks are quiet and as we pass a small bakery we make plans to stop here on the way back for some locally baked goods. It seems as though we are the only ones here on that mid-week morning in May. We know that we are getting closer to the site when we stumble across the small symbols of barbed wire painted onto the pavement that "guide us" to the entrance of Ravensbrück concentration camp, suggesting that this was also the main route for the 130,000 female prisoners to pass through.

There is no dramatic entrance to the camp; at least, not the way we have experienced before at other sites during this program. No groups of visitors assemble in large numbers in front of a large *Arbeit Macht Frei* sign to take photographs of what has become an iconic representation of camp sites, and as we would observe at Dachau or Auschwitz. If anything, the opposite is the case; there are neither large groups of visitors nor are we greeted by any visible symbolic representations of the Holocaust. The former camp site is "tucked away" in a seemingly residential area. There is a youth hostel and adjacent bike path in the vicinity of the former camp site which distracts us in our task of looking for recognizable camp structures. Students take note of the abandoned houses leading up to the camp entrance (they are looking at former SS residential quarters that are now vacant and desolate). There is a general sense of neglect of the space with wild vegetation along the paths. As we enter the camp grounds, we notice that it is just as empty as the streets that led us here. We seem to be the only visitors. No lines, no tourists, no security—all of which are common at, for instance, the Auschwitz memorial museum.[1] The students are visibly perplexed—by the vacant feel of the town, the unassuming entrance to the camp, and the empty camp itself. Something feels different about this site and it made an impact on the group: "*it [Ravensbrück] was very empty...but upon later reflection I felt that it was one of the most beautiful memorials I've ever seen.*"

THE HAUNTING QUALITIES OF RAVENSBRÜCK

In an attempt to find a vocabulary for our experiences at Ravensbrück and to acknowledge our personal reflections as a method of knowledge production—the fact that the camp defies our expectations starting from that moment we arrive at the train station to when we enter and subsequently experience the vacant space of the site itself—I am taking cues from the intriguing, and provocative, work of Jessica Auchter and Avery Gordon. Both authors advocate adopting the language of "ghostly" and "haunting" qualities to help us think through our encounters with memory and trauma.[2] Auchter convinces me to think about our experiences in terms of how some memorial sites "offer an interesting way to explore the questions of life and death through the politics of haunting."[3]

In the way it is understood here, "ghostly" does not necessarily refer to an activity of spirits (though this could be a consideration for future explorations). Rather, it is used as a tool to develop language and meaning to help us register the kinds of impressions and sensations that are otherwise incomprehensible to us. Take Gordon, for instance, who uses the concept of "ghostly" to meditate those moments when something that we may not see or know of creeps into our consciousness. That moment when we feel unsettled; when something familiar becomes foreign; when we may lose our bearings. I encourage my students to pause and reflect on these moments when "*things are not in their assigned places.*"[4] In a subsequent assignment, one student describes the "out-of-place" emotion she felt at Ravensbrück when "*never in my life have I felt such peace and calmness, which seems weird to say about a concentration camp.*" Another student writes more specifically about how the sensory features of the camp were at odds with what he knew about the history of, and thus expected from, the site: "*Upon arrival at Ravensbrück, I was taken aback at how beautiful and tranquil it all seemed. For a moment, I lost sight of the fact that I was standing on the ground where tens of thousands of women had perished.*"

These impressions do generally not leave us. They stay with us to "haunt" us: Gordon continues to note that these ghostly, unfamiliar qualities in an experience disturb our feelings, "cannot be put away" and, in that, they demand our attention.[5] The same student continues to write on his lasting impression of the camp: *"the entire place has given the Holocaust an entirely new meaning to me."*

So what is it that feels ghostly at Ravensbrück? What, or who, unsettles us? In thinking about the mechanisms that may help us to make intelligible our experience at Ravensbrück, I borrow from Auchter again who anchors the quality of what haunts us in the concept of absence; we are haunted, of course, by something or someone that is not present—but used to be. In her captivating work on *The Politics of Haunting and Memory in International Relations*, she directs our attention to the ways in which the concept of absence evokes hauntings, for instance, about the people whose loss we experience. But how is the concept of absence different at Ravensbrück than at other camps? In many ways, representations of absence are an encounter quite common to the Holocaust memorial landscape; take for instance the display of belongings at Auschwitz (piles of hairs, shoes, personal items), which evokes the absence of the people to whom they belonged.[6] As Auchter reminds us, "each shoe bears the trace of the absent body that lived and marked it."[7] When we think about sites of violence, this aesthetics of absence brings about two main, and interlinked, aspects of memorialization: It does not only speak to what *used* to be there/present, but it is also inextricably intertwined with the violence that produced the absence.[8]

I argue that at Ravensbrück the sense of what and who is absent, and what and who thus haunts us, is invoked through an intricate ensemble of characteristics in the built and social structures that are quite unique at the site (and the surroundings of the camp as I describe them at the outset of this chapter). The role of the grounds, the spaces that point to emptiness, the decaying and organic structures of the remaining buildings—all speak to the students' senses in impactful ways. A student writes:

> Ravensbrück has been the most thought-provoking concentration camp we've visited […] Perhaps it's because of its location, or maybe simply just because it lacks the same architectural remnants that many other concentration camp memorial sites possess, requiring imaginative ventures into unthinkable territory.

The largely empty camp site appears to reinforce its "content" without resorting to literal representations or explanations of the experience.[9]

In a 1997 lecture, Daniel Libeskind argued that the built environment and its structures "provides viewers with a unique experience of the materiality of trauma," emphasizing specifically the components of absence and loss.[10] Golanska speaks of the "aesthetic bodily experiences" that visitors to sites can have, and offers some specific readings of what those experiences may look like. Using the example of the Holocaust memorial site in Belzec, Poland, Golanska explains how the architectural construction of Belzec affects our senses, ranging from the visual play of light and shadow reflecting on the grounds to the sounds that echo off the surrounding walls.[11] These structures reiterate a sense of emptiness and loss, and through that, they also heighten our awareness of the lives that are now devoid of the place. As one student reflects, *"the camp was eerily empty, allowing for our voices to echo off of the very same walls that the victims had shouted in pain behind just 70 years prior. As we walked, the sound of shifting gravel filled the space."* The appeal to absence makes a deeply felt impact on my cohort and there is an overwhelming feeling of solitude and sadness that I notice among the group. One student admits that *"the lake was beautiful, and the town could be seen in the distance. The camp just felt so real to me."*

Gordon admits that haunting can be a frightening experience.[12] To notice the lives and bodies absent from the camp site means also to register the harm and injury inflicted in the past, leading to that absence in the present; "haunting always harbors violence that made it", Gordon explains.[13] The emptiness in the camp, for instance, the large empty area where the prisoner's wards once used to be or the vast area where the roll call used to be held, produces a very intimate experience as students struggle to reconcile the present emptiness with the fact that these spaces were once filled and cramped with female, suffering, bodies. *"It was a much more personal experience,"* says a student. Our sense of empty, yet symbolic spaces, is described beautifully by Landsberg who speaks of an "odd sense of intimacy with those people who are at an unbridgeable distance, who are conspicuously absent."[14] Students were receptive to this experience of hauntedness, concluding the day at Ravensbrück with saying that *"I could feel the victims around much more."*

Haunting as a concept also offers a promising starting point to think about the question of gendered experiences with regard to the Holocaust. Students remark how *"Ravensbrück was the most relevant to me, not only as a woman, but also because it served to open up the topic on how gender played its role in the Holocaust, something I had never before been forced to think about.*" Female students, in particular, reflect on their own vulnerabilities as women during our guided tour of the site, which is littered with narratives of the very specific emotional and physical experiences of the female prisoners in the camp. Of those narratives they write:

> the one that resonated with me most was the fact that these women were so malnourished for so long (which was obviously not true only for the women) that they stopped menstruating. This was often so severe that many of these women were infertile after they were freed, if they survived.

It was noted that this contributed significantly to "*an ability to personally empathize with the female prisoners*" and that "*concentrating on the female victims burdens and stories in the camp made it a much more emotional experience for me as a woman.*" In leading a group of students through the camp, I find that Ravensbrück is one of the most uncomfortable—haunting—explorations of human vulnerabilities and as illustrated through the female body/female experiences located there.

Vanishing Perpetrators

I suggested that the concept of haunting offers a valuable vocabulary for describing those instances that affect us deeply but for which we often lack a framework of understanding. However, haunting offers more. Returning to Gordon's work once again, she proposes another valuable insight that can come from thinking through the meaning of haunting; she puts it this way: "Haunting raises specters," she purports. These specters appear when "the trouble they represent or symptomize is no longer being contained or suppressed or blocked from view."[15] I read this to mean that if we allow ourselves to feel haunted by encouraging intricate, personal experiences with absence and loss, we may view "what's been in our blind spot" all along.[16] In the context of our visit at Ravensbrück, I encountered this with my students when they began making connections between the ghostly absence of the women at the camp and the ways in which these women were also missing from the larger memorial landscape in Germany and from their own knowledge about the specific role of female victims and perpetrators.

I often associate this transformation in my students' thinking with the tone of the short section in a book called *The Touch of the Past*. In that particularly memorable section, called "Why Vilna?", the authors make a case for the need to trace surviving testaments of the Vilna Ghetto in Lithuania in order to explore practices of remembrance central to Eastern Europe.[17] Against this backdrop, the question "*Why Vilna?*" [as in, "*Why focus on Vilna!?*"] is used to, at least partially, problematize our expectations about *where* violence occurred in the Holocaust. These only marginally include the ghettos of Eastern Europe. The authors are therefore drawn to Vilna to question these marginalizations of typologies of violence and demystify the topographies of Holocaust atrocity. To put it in the authors' words, Vilna serves as a "counter-response to the contemporary metonymic emphasis on Auschwitz as the reductive center of the Shoah."[18]

So with the objective of this excerpt in mind I, too, ask my students after our visit to the camp, "*Why Ravensbrück?*". The responses to that question can be summarized as follows; for some, the women's camp that is tucked away in the north of Berlin—similarly remote—acts as an interruption and a decentering of favored and dominant narratives of violence and victimhood in their knowledge of the Holocaust. It is what Gordon referred to as the process of exposing "what is in our blind spot."[19] Here, students speak of having learned "*an entirely new perspective into the lives of victims to, and perpetrators of, the Nazi regime,*" alluding here to a gendered lens not only to understand pain and suffering but also motivate to inflict such suffering. In this sense, "why Ravensbrück" is synonymous with asking "where are the women in our teaching and learning about the Holocaust?"

I am going back to the attentiveness to textures and spatial sensations that we experience at the site to suggest that they reinforce an awareness of the larger absence of women's narratives in learning about the Holocaust: "*we did not know that there was a women's camp,*" I hear one of my students say. To me, this raises a broader question for educators about how do we deal specifically with the representation of the perpetrators when teaching at sites of trauma and violence such as Ravensbrück. Students often begin this program with limited awareness of the complexity and enormity of human destructiveness. This needs to be understood in the context of two, further, questions: How do we deal with the role of perpetrators in our teaching of the Holocaust *in general?* And furthermore, how can the narrative of perpetrators be understood against the background of their representation in the (in this case, the German) memorial landscape?[20]

Admittedly, in my own teaching, I mostly ask students to look through the victims' lens; learning the intricate details of the lives of perpetrators, tracing their motivations, steps, thoughts—none of these occupy much space on my syllabus. One student reaction at Ravensbrück speaks to that lack of perpetrator knowledge:

> Rarely do we learn through the lens of the perpetrator; it is always through the lens of the victim. To see that these guards [at Ravensbrück] had families and lives and hobbies is something we often forget. The entire place has given the Holocaust a new meaning to me

How to "deal" with the perpetrators in educational programs has been debated among educators for many years.[21] The obvious question would be of course how one can teach about the Holocaust but "*not* confront the issue of the perpetrators?"[22] But as is evident in contemporary debates on Holocaust education, the voice of the perpetrator "has been largely marginalized."[23] There are obvious reasons for this; one has perhaps simply to do with the choices that we as educators have to make against the backdrop of limited curriculum time—if pressed for class time, the survivor's testimony is heard but less so the perpetrator's.[24]

Related to that is, a much more pressing reason, however, that has to do with the issue of the moral complexities when faced with perpetrator testimony, documentation, and evidence: Is it ethical to present perpetrators as witnesses to the Holocaust? And, while contributions such as Goldhagen's *Willing Executioners,* Browning's *Ordinary Men,* Littell's *The Kindly Ones,* or Fein's *The Calculus of Genocide* have clearly added to the critical imperative to understand the motivations and complexities of historical actors as perpetrators, such understanding is for educators often pitched against the moral imperative not to rationalize perpetrators' acts.[25] The same ethical turmoil exists of course at memorial sites, such as former concentration camps. It is "quite understandable," writes Heyl, that survivors "claim for themselves the scenes of the crimes as places of remembrance and there is something to their concern that a more detailed presentation of the perpetrators would take away (exhibition) space from the commemoration of those who were murdered."[26] This means, therefore, that in German discourse of commemoration, "places with a historical connection to the crimes of the Nazis are divided into those associated with perpetrators and those associated with victims."[27] There are only a few sites on our itinerary that are solely devoted to confronting the spaces of perpetrators. The House of the Wannsee Conference (Villa Wannsee) comes to mind, the noble estate outside Berlin where the heads of the most important government ministries were brought together to present their thoughts and ideas for the formal organization and execution of the *Final Solution*. We also cover the realm of individual perpetrators when we trace Hitler's rise to power during out stay in Munich, and Adolf Eichmann's role in the conceptualization of perpetrators through Hannah Arendt's thoughts on the banality of evil (this is usually folded into our visit to Nuremberg and questions of the role of trials).

This seemingly dichotomous model of teaching and learning about perpetrators and victims has been on the radar for educators for quite some time. It is indicative of the much larger complexities of the German memorial landscape within which programs and museum sites are deeply embedded. Heyl provides a brief, yet insightful, journey through some of these complexities; a striking example here is the ways in which Germans largely treated the history of Nazism in a third person, passive, narrative which resulted in speaking inevitably about the victims but did not provide language for talking about the perpetrators.[28] There have been significant attempts to shift this perspective and to problematize the fact that it is easier to sympathize with the victims than it is to trace how "ordinary people" may become perpetrators. I would not go as far as to accommodate suggestions that students should sympathize also with perpetrators but I certainly discuss with students the dangers of vanishing perpetrator perspectives in educational and other settings.[29]

The Ravensbrück memorial site gestures at these complexities. While attempts to commemorate the victims without reference to their perpetrators is impossible—"they are the core, after all, of the entire catastrophe"[30]—any specificity and depth about the perpetrators that may perhaps even lead to identifying with them is insensitive, or even dangerous (there is always concern about attracting neo-Nazis and turning former sites into pilgrimages).[31] In this context, Ravensbrück *is* a place where the lives of perpetrators who committed their crimes are discussed in detail, while it is also a place of commemoration for the victims. In fact, and as student noticed on the walk toward the camp the immediate impression one gets is that "perpetrator buildings"—such as the former SS residential quarters we pass by—dominate the memorial site. The youth hostel that we were initially distracted by when arriving at the camp is what used to be the living quarters of the camp guards. The centrality of the remnants of the abhorrent acts of female perpetrators aids students in unpacking the complexities of perpetrators' motivations and narratives. It adds significantly to the overall study of perpetrators by "challenging the notion of simplified 'types' of Nazi perpetrator, by shedding light on 'ordinary' perpetrators."[32] Students support this by noting *"rarely do we learn through the lens of the perpetrator, it is always through that if the victim. To see that these guards had families and lives and hobbies, it's something we often forget. The entire place has given the Holocaust an entirely new meaning to me."*

In closing, in subsequent reflections, most students of them will take away an appreciation of what the insight of women's experiences can add to their knowledge about the Holocaust. One student puts it this way:

> I believe Ravensbrück to be one of the most relevant memorial sights I have seen, not only on this trip but also perhaps in my entire life. [It] thoroughly deepened my understanding of how gender did play a very significant role in the Holocaust, in terms of both victims and perpetrators alike.

To us, Ravensbrück is a haunted place. It is haunted not only by the ghosts of female victims but also female perpetrators that have been marginalized in the narratives when teaching the Holocaust. Students query this,

> another aspect of the women's camp was the idea of female perpetrators that was not as obvious elsewhere during the Holocaust. It is very difficult for humankind to comprehend female perpetrators because the gender norms do not view women as a group who is capable of violence and murder.

Auchter begins her study on encounters of hauntedness with a nod to an important premise: One needs to allow oneself to be haunted. This has to do with what lies at the very core of the concept of haunted: it may not end; after all, "endings that are not over is what haunting is about."[33] There is something incredibly powerful about my students' intricate processing of their reflections as ghostly and haunting experiences. I encourage them to explore and nourish those reflections fully and with an eye on two main learning objectives. Initially, I would describe students' reflections on Ravensbrück as a transformative experience that gives possibility toward a more nuanced understanding of the

Holocaust. The numerous quotes I injected into this chapter should be an indication of that. The rhetoric of gender-specific and bodily experiences added an additional layer of knowledge that complicated students' neat and packaged understanding of the violence suffered during the Holocaust. The representations of the systematic and mass killings—as integral as they must be in our teaching—are often out of reach for students and suffer from a vocabulary of abstraction. They are certainly not reflective of the intricacies of individual and subjective narratives of suffering and pain. In countering this, the personal experiences of female prisoners are accessible to students and they weave these individual stories into their own personal (gendered) lives.

But feeling haunted is productive in other ways; it is not a passive experience but can be seen as a state of resistance.[34] Witnessing involves more than looking on. Gordon notes that "haunting, *unlike* trauma, is distinctive for producing a something-to-be-done."[35] But what may that be? Initially, I would suggest that it "does" allow students to feel uprooted, and by recognizing the absence of certain, taken-for-granted representations and narratives we begin resisting the symbolic representations of the Holocaust that we often travel through. Daniel Libeskind speaks of "unsettling spaces" that imply that the viewer cannot remain in a distant, seemingly safe position of spectatorship.[36] Students start to defy the singularity of violence and instead opt to include a multiperspectivity that includes the study of perpetrators.

Lastly, letting someone or something haunt us through a personal experience (in this case, some of the female, bodily experiences that students learned about) is part of developing a sense of what it means to an engaged, caring, and committed individual in the face of ongoing challenges. When I say "ongoing", I am reminded of a more recent representation of an atrocity through the concept of absence: Michael Arad and Peter Walker's design for the National 9/11 Memorial at Ground Zero—*Reflecting Absence*. Two deeply recessed voids can be found now in the footprints of the former World Trade Center towers with thin veils of water cascading into reflecting pools; each with further deep voids in its middle.[37] While this is of course not a Holocaust memorial its preoccupation with "loss, absence and regeneration" may well be informed by Holocaust memory, Young argues.[38] The designers arrived at this creation with the question on how to articulate absence and void without "fixing" and filling it? How to "formalize irreparable loss without seeming to repair it"?[39] For Young, this has been achieved with *Reflecting Absence* because it is not reduced to historicizing an event but instead it leaves open the void to some extent. This "never-to-be-completed" process is generative for it animates debates, arguments, and tensions. We, too, leave Ravensbrück with that "never-to-be-completed" sentiment, for which I used the concept of haunting in the writings here. The former camp site resists turning visitors and students into passive spectators. Instead, it invites us to recognize and probe competing memorial agendas, and be suspicious of attempts to "fix and repair" absence that may result in the marginalization of some (here female) voices.

NOTES

1. Auschwitz-Birkenau News (2015) "Growing attendance and security at the Memorial," Available: http://auschwitz.org/en/museum/news/growing-attendance-and-security-at-the-memorial,1147.html. Accessed July 1, 2016.
2. Auchter, J. (2014) *The Politics of Haunting and Memory in International Relations* (Routledge).
3. Auchter, *The Politics of Haunting and Memory in International Relations*, p. 2.
4. Gordon, A. (2008) *Ghostly Matters: Haunting and the Sociological Imagination*, (Minneapolis, MN: University of Minnesota Press), p. xvi.
5. Gordon, *Ghostly Matters: Haunting and the Sociological Imagination*, p. xvi.
6. Auchter, *The Politics of Haunting and Memory in International Relations*.
7. Landsberg, A. (2004) *Prosthetic Memory: The Age of Transformation of American Remembrance in the Age of Mass Culture*, (Columbia University Press), p. 134.
8. Auchter, *The Politics of Haunting and Memory in International Relations*, p. 127.
9. Golanska, D. (2015) "Affective Spaces, Sensuous Engagements: In Quest of a Synaesthetic Approach to 'Dark Memorials'," *International Journal of Heritage Studies*, 21:8, 773–790.
10. Heckner, E. (2008) "Whose Trauma is it?", in Bathrick, D., Prager, B, and Richardsen, M. (Eds.) *Visualizing the Holocaust. Documents, Aesthetics*, Memory (New York: Camden House), pp. 62–85, p. 63.
11. Golanska, "Affective Spaces, Sensuous Engagements: In Quest of a Synaesthetic Approach to 'Dark Memorials'", p. 780.
12. Gordon, *Ghostly Matters: Haunting and the Sociological Imagination*.

13. Gordon, *Ghostly Matters: Haunting and the Sociological Imagination*, p. 207.
14. Landsberg, *Prosthetic Memory: The Age of Transformation of American Remembrance in the Age of Mass Culture'*, p. 133.
15. Gordon, *Ghostly Matters: Haunting and the Sociological Imagination*, p. xvi.
16. Gordon, *Ghostly Matters: Haunting and the Sociological Imagination*, p. xvi.
17. Simon, R (2005) *The Touch of the Past. Remembrance, Learning and Ethics* (Palgrave Macmillan), pp. 107–110.
18. Simon, *The Touch of the Past. Remembrance, Learning and Ethics*, p. 107.
19. Gordon, *Ghostly Matters: Haunting and the Sociological Imagination*, p. xvi.
20. Heyl, M. (2009) "Teaching and Learning about Perpetrators within Memorial Sites," Conference Contribution *Perpetrator Research in a Global Context*, Available: http://www.bpb.de/veranstaltungen/doku-mentation/127465/perpetrator-research-in-a-global-context-taeter-forschung-im-globalen-kontext. Accessed May 15, 2015.
21. Heyl, "Teaching and Learning about Perpetrators within Memorial Sites".
22. Zeitlin, F. (2004) "Teaching about Perpetrators," in Hirsch, M. and Kacandes, I. (eds) *Teaching the Representation of the Holocaust* (New York: Modern Language Association of America), p. 69.
23. Gray, M. (2014) *Contemporary Debates in Holocaust Education*, (UK: Palgrave MacMillan), p. 92.
24. Gray, *Contemporary Debates in Holocaust Education*.
25. Goldhagen, D. (1975) *Hitler's Willing Executioners* (Alfred Knopf) Browning, C. (1992) *Ordinary Men: Reserve Police Battalion 101 and the Final Solution in Poland*, (Harper Perennial). Littell, J. (2006) *The Kindly Ones*, (HarperCollins).
26. Heyl, "Teaching and Learning about Perpetrators within Memorial Sites," p. 3.
27. Heyl, "Teaching and Learning about Perpetrators within Memorial Sites," p. 1.
28. Heyl, "Teaching and Learning about Perpetrators within Memorial Sites," p. 3.
29. Bormann, N. (2016) "The Importance of Remembering Nazi Perpetrators," *E-IR*, Available: www.e-ir.info/2016/09/14/the-importance-of-remembering-nazi-perpetrators/.
30. Zeitlin, "Teaching about perpetrators," p. 69.
31. Heyl, M. (1997) *Erziehung nach Auschwitz. Eine Bestandsaufnahme* (Kraemer Verlag).
32. Harvey, E. (2009) "Women as perpetrators," Conference Contribution *Perpetrator Research in a Global Context*, Available: http://www.bpb.

de/veranstaltungen/dokumentation/127465/perpetrator-research-in-a-global-context-taeterforschung-im-globalen-kontext. Accessed 15 May 2015.

33. Gordon, *Ghostly Matters*, p. 139.
34. Auchter, *The Politics of Haunting and Memory in International Relations.*
35. Gordon, *Ghostly Matters*, p. xvi.
36. Heckner, E. (2008) "Whose Trauma is it?", in Bathrick, D., Prager, B, and Richardsen, M. (Eds.) *Visualizing the Holocaust. Documents, Aesthetics*, Memory (New York: Camden House), pp. 62–85.
37. Young, J. (2016) "The memorial's arc: Between Berlin's Denkmal and New York City's 9/11 Memorial," *Memory Studies*, 9:3, 325–331.
38. Young, "The memorial's arc: Between Berlin's Denkmal and New York City's 9/11 Memorial," p. 326.
39. Young, "The memorial's arc: Between Berlin's Denkmal and New York City's 9/11 Memorial," p. 325.

CHAPTER 5

"*My Therapist Told Me not to Visit Auschwitz*": The Problem with crisis pedagogy

Abstract That the teaching of a topic that principally deals with mass atrocity, death, and annihilation has the potential to produce a set of powerful feelings is perhaps self-evident. But what the exact nature of these feelings is, how to foresee them, and how to mediate and deal with them is far more complex and difficult. Surveys at sites of trauma and violence have shown that visitors predominantly encounter negative emotions during their presence at sites and that these feelings may have long-lasting effects. This should raise some serious ethical concerns for educators whose students may experience feelings of shock, sadness, and anxiety in their encounter with the material. The structure of a five-week long study abroad program can significantly intensify students' emotional experience; the intimacy with the material at sites of trauma and violence can be particularly burdensome and is compounded by the length of the program, the quantity of sites visited, and the length of time spent at sites. This chapter narrates the emotions reported by my students at sites and contextualizes them within the debates on the effect of vicarious experiences on compassion and empathy. Underscoring the importance of students' intimate understanding of the material, I offer a set of suggestions on a more controlled engagement with the traumatic effects of "being there."

Keywords Vicarious suffering · Compassion · Empathy · Emotions Trauma

It should be clear by now, and from the encounters described in the previous chapters, that teaching and learning at former sites of trauma and violence provides the learner with many cognitive, reflective, and experiential opportunities. This also means, visits are emotionally laden and more often than not susceptible to creating "emotionally fraught situations" for both student and educator.[1] Some of those fraught situations are at the core of the stories told on the previous pages, and include students' affective response to atrocity footage; the intricate personal experiences of loss and absence that I characterized as haunting and ghostly; and also the difficulties in navigating the charge of dark or trauma tourism. This chapter seeks to add another layer—what learners themselves "bring" to the program, and how that impacts their learning at sites. This may include prior knowledge about the Holocaust itself; expectations and assumptions about the sites we subsequently visit; but also students' well-being and emotional resilience that equip them to absorb and manage the often graphic and shocking representations of atrocity.

It seems perhaps obvious to note that there has been a long-standing commitment by scholars and educators alike to chart the potential traumatic effects and emotional imprint that follows from visiting sites of violence and suffering. Chapter 3 was at pains to query how the affective responses may translate into measurable outcomes. This is especially clear in discussions on the politics of photography; I carved out a small part of that scholarship in an attempt to tackle some of the methodological dilemmas posed by the use of graphic atrocity imagery in Holocaust education, for instance. In that context, I borrowed largely from visual cultural studies and the discipline of international relations, both of which offer valuable insights with regard to the impact of our gaze at atrocity photographs and films; "what do images really do?" was the main question weaving through my observation of my students' gaze. While the exact nature of the audience uptake is, in fact, unclear—both affect and efficacy remain speculative at best—there are nonetheless valuable methodologies in place to engage with the "visual turn" in the study of genocide and atrocity. Those gesture toward adopting a "multi-method approach" in general[2] as well as an emphasis on cultivating students' self-reflexivity and their understanding of the politics of spectatorship in particular.[3]

I have always had strong feelings about the (ab)use of atrocity imagery—the "shock value"—in Holocaust education in general and the potential traumatizing affect that may come with that for my students

in particular. With that being said, some of the methodological suggestions within the realm of ethical spectatorship raised in this book have
become a firmly anchored principle in my teaching pedagogy at sites
of trauma. But when one of my students confides in me that her thera-
pist had cautioned her against visiting the former Nazi death camp of
Auschwitz-Birkenau due to existing health concerns, I begin to feel that
my grasp on those methodologies slips. I start to worry about the (ethical) implications of traumatizing my students on this journey. How can
I realistically mediate students' personal health during a five-week inten-
sive program that is bound to (and ought to) challenge students in their
emotions? What practices should I adopt that take into consideration not
only what meets us at the sites, and the Holocaust as an event, but also
the emotional resilience of students?

FEELING WHAT WE SEE

There is a common wisdom in Holocaust education on the centrality of
deep emotional experiences as a key component in classroom teaching.
This has to do with the proposition that only after (or with) an emotional experience can the intellectual understanding follow; partially,
because "central to understanding the event intellectually is understanding the impossibility of its being fully understood, a realization that has
an emotional (or visceral) component."[4] For educators, this inexorably
translates into a fundamental question: "if we want students to "never
forget," must they have an unforgettable [emotional] experience?".[5] For
Alsup, this question signals essentially a dilemma: How far can pedagogy
instruct trauma? And do students need to experience some kind of emotional crisis in order to comprehend the crisis of the event?[6]

There are only few studies that empirically investigate visitors' emotions at sites of trauma and violence.[7] Those are mostly descriptive and
emotions experienced range from sadness and fear to anguish and sorrow. There is interview material conducted with young visitors to
Auschwitz[8] and genocide sites in general[9]; they, too, reveal emotions of
sadness or disgust. While studies are limited, it would be fair to say that
negative emotions (such as shock and horror) seem to dominate positive ones (such as hope). Some purport that these negative emotions are
of particular importance in that they "may have long term behavioral
consequences."[10] Again, what those consequences may look like is also
ambiguous. However, most of these studies are qualitative in nature and

focus on the *kinds* of emotions in visitors, less so the intensity within which those were experienced.[11]

With those existing explorations in mind, I began surveying how my students see and notice the emotional impact that being at sites has on them, and in the context of the overall program. During our debrief session at the end of the program, I engaged the group in thinking about how they would "describe their emotional experience" and if they felt it impacted on their personal health. Most of the students' reflections on their emotional well-being referenced the direct, intimate, experience as witnesses to the atrocities of the Holocaust at the sites themselves. Students survey their emotional response to our visits with words such as "*heart-wrenching*," "*claustrophobic*," and "*horror*." They speak of their experience as "*completely overwhelming*," and often "*being moved to tears*." At the end of a long list of lived emotional responses along the lines of "*sad*," "*scary*," and "*horribly tragic*," one student writes, "*I looked at my professor asking—really?*".

These experiences described here are commonly subsumed into the concepts of vicarious experiences, or vicarious trauma, and secondary witnessing—best understood as a (re)experiencing a traumatic event not as a first-hand survivor but through reading and viewing Holocaust texts, images, and testimonies.[12] The triggers of such vicarious trauma have been sketched in the previous two chapters on haunting and the use of atrocity imagery. The ways in which traumatic experiences of visitors is valued as productive and important is most poignantly explored through the eyes of Daniel Libeskind. Using the Jewish Museum in Berlin as an example, Libeskind was at pains to create an architectural design that would engage visitors in "emotional and visceral ways" and with the aim to "capture a physical and spatial, even bodily experience of trauma instead of offering representations intended to appeal solely to the intellect."[13]

Where does this traumatic experience "go"; why does it matter? Intimacy, the argument goes, facilitates compassion. The work of Marianne Hirsch is clearly central in unpacking the relationship between our visceral experience of trauma and how it relates to our own being and acting. Hirsch insists that our entering of a space of trauma (literally and figuratively) "will have transformative effects on those who did not experience the Holocaust."[14] How so? Johnson looks to Arendt who provides an answer; she rightly suggests that compassion involves sharing the pain or misery—*literally the passion*—of another so intensely as to engender a sort of vicarious experience of suffering.[15]

The absorbing of someone else's trauma contains a double-edged sword for educators. One the one hand, and adopting Libeskind dictum, central to the conception of witnessing trauma is the notion of physically "being in" the space of trauma versus discursively addressing it.[16] Think of the display of personal items of the victims of the Holocaust at the Auschwitz memorial museum—large spaces filled with hair and shoes— that has become a familiar example for the ways in which to evoke an extremely emotional response. Another example used in this book is the experience of the vast space of the grounds at Auschwitz-Birkenau that is reflective of the scale and industrialized mechanisms of destruction. We encounter the materiality of trauma most effectively, Libeskind insists, by "walking, by looking, by touching, by feeling *where* one is."[17] However, and on the other hand, without interpretation, explanation, and discursively addressing it, students as visitors may never move beyond this emotive reaction. Without context, the items on display appear as a spectacle; as Lennon and Foley note, there is "almost complete absence of any commentary upon the objects themselves, thereby trusting the visitor to analyze and evaluate the exhibits."[18] This side of the double edged sword asks, therefore, how far we then discursively engage. How much do we, as educators, prepare, guide, and interpret the material encountered at sites? I turn to Hirsch on this who draws us into a discussion on the centrality of compassion —to mean to adopt someone else's trauma as one's own — but at the same time cautions us from getting dangerously close to such moments. Hirsch is skeptical, to put it mildly, about attempts to enact anything akin to an "identificatory model of Holocaust education."[19] In other words, while our visceral experience is perhaps crucial to our empathetic understanding of the suffering endured by others, we must retain some distance to that suffering and abstain from a teaching model that insinuate that we can in fact fully explore, or simulate, that suffering. Dauphinee offers an intricate analysis of the fraught relationship between other body's pain and our gaze of it; she states, "the act of witnessing others' pain (and deaths) is also fraught with an unsay-ability, because the witness is limited to only a modicum of access to the trauma of the other body."[20] My mind wanders back to our guide at Auschwitz-Birkenau who would preface our walk along some of the sections of the grounds with "*now you are walking to the gas chambers the same way the prisoners did.*"

Beyond the dilemma of this double-edged sword of how vicarious experiences can be channeled and curated by educators to develop into feelings of compassion, there is, of course, larger criticism in place that must be considered. The concept of compassion entraps many critics and commentators: Compassion is, as Susan Sontag sees it, "an unstable condition."[21] Sontag piercingly asks: "The question is what to do with the feelings that have been aroused, the knowledge that has been communicated. If one feels there is nothing 'we' can do [...] – then one starts to get bored, cynical, apathetic."[22] Frankly, emotional responses may "bring us up short."[23] Some of my students' experiences feel arresting precisely because "the moment of the other's suffering engulfs us". In other words, what we see, read, and feel generate compassion and empathy in the learner. *However*, that feeling is "unexpectedly perverse" because the past suffering that we are witness to is well past any possible remedy.[24] There is no purchase to our compassion and it can readily induce hopelessness and a feeling of personal moral inadequacy.[25]

This is confirmed through some of the other comments made by students in response to my surveying of their emotional health: Others felt less of a visceral reaction that often accompany the experiences at sites; rather, they noted feeling *"anxious"* by the demands that the atrocities placed upon them but to which they could not respond. It would appear that the more they witnessed and saw, the more they were overcome with the burden of acting on that knowledge; feeling *"overburdened by knowledge"* is an often-exclaimed expression during the program. A student specified, *"the responsibility felt about the Holocaust and knowledge about it caused stress."*

When asked by my colleagues about what I would describe as the most challenging aspect of this program, pedagogically speaking, I always retort to Hirsch's notion of "controlled retraumatization."[26] I read Hirsch's phrase not to mean that my students' experiences can, in fact, be scripted or controlled, but rather that their affective encounters should be confined to a "momentary affect" and couched within other, safe and distant, structures and experience.[27] And so, specifically, the challenge is not posed by attempting *not* to expose students to moments of hurt and trauma but by offering relief and distance to reflect and work through those moments. Ezra speaks here aptly of the tension created "by the double vision required by a pedagogy of hurt and hope."[28] This means, thinking about ways in which we can create an experience around the hurt of the Holocaust that does not dwell so much on hurt that we cause violence to our students. It should also include structures to allow for students to have a safe distance, especially when taking into consideration the injuries and challenges they themselves inhabit in their personal lives.

Feeling Safe: Controlling Traumatic Affect

I want to return to Hirsch again for a moment who makes two significant arguments regarding the role of traumatic effects. I see these as reminders on how to think carefully about the perilous effects of strong associations that my students may have with the suffering of others. One argument calls for resisting "annihilating the distance between the self and other, the otherness of the other."[29] This can be seen as a call for establishing an emotional-affective tie to the victims of the Holocaust (and this is crucial, in turn, for establishing an ethical spectatorship).[30] The other argument underscores the importance of being able to find some distance from these affective experiences and to have an opportunity to "turn away" from the "injurious power of traumatic affect."[31]

To argue that balancing these two arguments can unleash a challenge for educators would be an understatement. In planning this program, I worry about how students will not only cope with the emotionally charged components of visits to sites and museums, but also the aggregate of these visits and confrontations over the course of five weeks; Hirsch's suggestion of "turning away" may be difficult to implement. I am left with the question on how to facilitate deep thinking and feeling while being responsive to the discomfort that this experience may cause to students. In the following, I want to outline a set of suggestions and strategies for tailoring a program that meets students' interests, needs, and location.

In thinking through some strategies, I am inspired by my students' suggestions. Those individuals who reported in our debrief session that they *did not* feel exposed to stressful situations and would not ascribe to feeling emotionally overwhelmed gave the *"highly structured"* and *"thought-through"* nature of the program as a reason. Knowing ahead of time what was expected of them was a key component of that sentiment, especially in terms of time frames for visits to sites and other essential organizational features—when assignments are due; when there is time to decompress; when they need to prepare leading up to a visit. The importance of some fundamental organizational structures that create transparency for students, and to being able to communicate those is not to be underestimated; in his reflections on the preparations for educational visits to the state museum at Majdanek, Kranz speaks of the relevance of supplementing reflections on educational effects at sites with some essential practical components.[32] We often lose sight of those components in light of emotive nature of the program. I make sure that expectations about the program—from our daily activities to student assignments—are as clear as possible and circulate an itinerary ahead of time that is updated regularly and meticulously throughout the program.

Some students also shared that they *"felt safe"* and that there is a strong appeal to feeling safe during the program. To me, this speaks strongly to Hirsch's notion of an ability to "turn away." While it is difficult, if not impossible, to monitor or control students' experiences when we are at the sites themselves, I can ensure that their time outside those site visits does function as an opportunity for turning away. I handpick the hotels we stay in and do so with the requirement that they are located in safe environments, offer a quiet space, and give students an opportunity to return to a comfortable and nurturing setting at the end of their study days. In preparation for departure on this program, I frequently invite an expert on trauma to speak to my study abroad group. This individual (this has been either a medical professional and/or a colleague on campus with experiences of visiting sites and places of suffering and trauma) shares with the group advice on how to stay healthy during the program; to avoid physical fatigue; to learn to communicate discomfort and anxieties; and to make and articulate choices about engagement with the material. These suggestions range from very practical ones—to stay hydrated when spending a long day on former camp grounds that can make us feel depleted and uncomfortable—to learn to engage in reflective writing exercises in order to comprehend the impressions of the day and meditative practices. The importance of transparency of schedules and activities plays a role here again, as students seek to know when they can engage in activities that help them to decompress from the encounters at the sites. Students noted that *"free time was helpful"* and gestured toward the importance of, as they put it, *"unloading the experiences of the day."* Most students specifically pointed to the ability to have group dinners and articulated the *"necessity to move on"* at the end of their days. In relation to their ability to interact with their peers in ways that help them navigate the emotional component of the program, students agreed that *"groups should be smaller."*

Having these very discussions and creating an environment where there is an openness of these procedures and mechanisms (such as through pre-departure meetings that we hold in preparation for our program) plays a central role for students' perceptions of the program itself. Students have commented that they appreciate *knowing* that their instructor's concern is with their physical and mental well-being which tells them something about "*the level of caring*" that they can rely on during the journey.

The most obvious techniques used to help students process the mate rial that we collect and experience during the day are writing exercises.[33] Assignments consist mostly of reflective essay writing which includes writing journal/blog entries and assignments geared toward folding the daily reflections into a particular historic or political event related to the site visited. I encourage students to write their papers at the end of the activity of the day and factor this time into the scheduling of the program.

However, some of the emotional experiences encountered cannot be addressed or met and lie beyond the scope of this program. Revisiting the concept of haunting once more, it should be clear that some of the emotions felt during this program will not leave the students. Many participants report that the "*emotional depth*" of the program came through "*when interacting with others back home.*" Students lament quite often that their choice in participating in a (summer) program of such depth is questioned by friends and family—before as well as after the program. "*Why would you do that,*" is the question frequently asked. Students agree that they lack the vocabulary to convey their interest in, and passion for, learning about the Holocaust without being cast as a trauma tourist.

There is no doubt in my mind that students' emotional well-being and resilience will continue to pose a unique challenge to Holocaust education at historic sites. I would argue that such a challenge might be compounded by the fact that students' mental health is being increasingly scrutinized. The growing chatter about the status of mental health on college and university campuses nationwide has certainly added to the conversation of the relationship and delicacy between pedagogy and trauma.[34] Given the visual nature of much of contemporary politics that contain a dizzying amount of imagery of suffering, pain, and mass murder, those preoccupations with mental health will (rightly) continue. This may be even further complicated by a sense of burgeoning reliance on the vocabulary of shock and horror at some of the sites we encounter, and as I narrated in Chap. 3 of this book.

Taken together this means that encouraging an emotive experience in students is much more complicated than it may appear. There is a swelling responsibility for educators to think about how they can craft an experience at sites that might "fit" students' needs and meets them where they are—emotionally and mentally.

By way of offering a final reflection on these thoughts, it is important to accept that we may never be able to anticipate students' emotional reactions; the when, where, and how of affect. That there is hesitation and anxiety felt prior to a visit to a death camp is perhaps to be expected, but most of the encounters that I observe come in fact unexpectedly. As such, they cannot be predicted, avoided, or manipulated—nor should they. But what we can do, and I follow Alsup on this, is to have "an awareness of and sensitivity to students' past educational and personal experiences."[35] One of the most moving written reflections submitted by one student illustrates this, and is aptly entitled *"an unexpected perspective."* In this reflection paper, students were tasked with reviewing their experiences in one section of the program—the sites and memorials in Berlin—and to choose, and justify, the memorial site that spoke to them the most. This particular student begins the paper by listing the kinds of memorials that one would expect to be powerfully moved by but then notes that *"none of these memorials evoked the emotion that the memorial to the victims of euthanasia did."* The student explains that she has been able to *"look somewhat objectively at the Holocaust [...] with no obvious personal ties to the victims."* The memorial to the victims of euthanasia, however, disrupted that distance for her; the personal biographies that the memorial displays connected with her because someone she deeply cares about with a mental health disease *"would have been deemed unfit for life and killed under the Nazi regime based on."* In an emotional concluding paragraph, the student admits that this encounter was *"so personally relevant because at all other memorials I have had feelings of humility and admiration, yet nowhere had I really felt fear. This fear challenged me"*.

NOTES

1. Wysok, W. (2013) "The principles of cooperation between museum pedagogical staff at memorial sites and teachers in carrying out educational projects—practical remarks," in Thomas Kranz et al. (Eds.) *The Purpose of Visiting Sties of Trauma in Education.*

2. Bleiker, R. (2015) "Pluralist Methods for Visual Global Politics," *Millennium*, 43:3, 872–890.
3. Adelman, R. (2014) "Atrocity and Aporiae: Teaching the Abu Ghraib Images, Teaching Against Transparency," *Cultural Studies—Critical Methodologies*, 14:1, 29–39.
4. Alsup, J. (2003) "A Pedagogy of Trauma," in Bernard-Donals, M. and Glejzer, R. (Eds.) *Witnessing the Disaster* (The University of Wisconsin Press), pp. 75–89, p. 88.
5. Alsup, "A Pedagogy of Trauma."
6. Alsup, "A Pedagogy of Trauma," p. 76.
7. Nawijn, J. and Fricke, M.-C. (2015) "Visitor Emotions and Behavioral Intentions: The Case of Concentration Camp Memorial Neuengamme", *International Journal of Tourism Research*, 17:3, 221–228.
8. Thurnell-Read, T. (2009) "Engaging Auschwitz: an analysis of young travellers' experiences of Holocaust tourism," *Journal of Tourism Consumption and Practice* 1(1): 26–52.
9. Sharpley R. (2012) "Towards and understanding of 'Genocide Tourism': an analysis of visitors' accounts of their experience of recent genocide sites," in Sharpley, R. and Stone, P. (Eds.) *Contemporary Tourist Experience: Concepts and Consequences* (Abingdon: Routledge), pp. 95–109.
10. Nawijn and Fricke, "Visitor Emotions and Behavioral Intentions: The Case of Concentration Camp Memorial Neuengamme."
11. Nawijn and Fricke, "Visitor Emotions and Behavioral Intentions: The Case of Concentration Camp Memorial Neuengamme."
12. Alsup, "A Pedagogy of Trauma."
13. Heckner, E. (2008) "Whose Trauma is it?", in Bathrick, D., Prager, B., and Richardson, M. (Eds.) *Visualizing the Holocaust. Documents, Aesthetics, Memory* (New York: Camden House), pp. 62–85, p. 63.
14. Heckner, E. (2008) "Whose Trauma is it?".
15. Johnson, J. (2011) "The Arithmetic of Compassion: Rethinking the Politics of Photography," *British Journal of Political Science*, 41:3, 621–643.
16. Heckner, "Whose Trauma is it?", p. 71.
17. Heckner, "Whose Trauma is it?", p. 73.
18. Lennon, J., and Foley, M. (2000) *Dark tourism: The attraction of death and disaster* (New York, NY: Continuum), p. 25.
19. Heckner, "Whose Trauma is it?", p. 65.
20. Dauphinee, E. (2007) "The Politics of the Body in Pain," *Security Dialogue*, 38:2, 139–155, p. 142.
21. Sontag, S. (2003) *Regarding the Pain of Others*, (Farrar, Straus and Giroux), p. 101.
22. Sontag, *Regarding the Pain of Others*, p. 101.
23. Johnson, J. (2011) "The Arithmetic of Compassion: Rethinking the Politics of Photography," *British Journal of Political Science* 41:3, 621–643.

24. Johnson, "The Arithmetic of Compassion': Rethinking the Politics of Photography," p. 623.
25. Johnson, "The Arithmetic of Compassion': Rethinking the Politics of Photography."
26. Heckner, "Whose Trauma is it?", p. 70.
27. Heckner, "Whose Trauma is it?".
28. Ezra, E. (2014) "A Pedagogy of Empathy for a World of Atrocity," *Review of Education, Pedagogy, and Cultural Studies*, 36:5, 343–371, p. 343.
29. Hirsch, M. (2001) "Surviving Images: Holocaust Photographs and the Work of Postmemory," *The Yale Journal of Criticism*, 14:1, 5–37, p. 221.
30. Heckner, "Whose Trauma is it?", p. 78.
31. Heckner, "Whose Trauma is it?", p. 70.
32. Kranz, T. (2013) *Educational Visits to the State Museum at Majdanek—A Guide for Teachers*, (Lublin : Państwowe Muzeum na Majdanku).
33. Apsel, J. (2004) "Moral Dilemmas and Pedagogical Challenges in Teaching about Genocide," *Human Rights Review*, 5:4, 104–129. p. 123).
34. Lukianoff, G. and Haidt, J. (2015) "The Coddling of the American Mind," *The Atlantic*, Available https://www.theatlantic.com/magazine/archive/2015/09/the-coddling-of-the-american-mind/399356/. Accessed 20 March 2016.
35. Alsup, "A Pedagogy of Trauma," p. 88.

CHAPTER 6

Conclusions: Looking Back at a Holocaust study abroad program

Abstract The concept of haunting has been an exceptionally rewarding framework for illuminating the kinds of encounters my group of students and I have experienced over the years at sites that are witness to what Jameson so eloquently termed the "hurts of history." "Haunting" has given us a language to apprehend and interpret our mental, emotional, and visceral experiences and to appreciate the transformative effect of those experiences—the very meaning of feeling haunted means that our encounters will stay with us long after the program's ending.

Keywords Haunting · Holocaust · Jameson · Hurts of history

~ *"Being haunted at every turn"* ~ This book has seen many quotes, reflections, and wonderfully intricate observations by the students I travelled with over the years. The opening quote to these final pages, however, is mine and encapsulates my own reflection on leading a Holocaust study abroad program. The emotional component of teaching the Holocaust, the experience of "being there" (at authentic sites) and "being in" (in places of trauma) has always been very real to me. Growing up in Germany and set amidst a landscape of shame and guilt, returning to these sites of violence, again and again, has been a very personal journey, and a difficult one at that. The most challenging—haunting—encounter from where I stand does not involve the narratives and graphic representations of mass atrocity and violence that so viscerally affect my students

N. Bormann, *The Ethics of Teaching at Sites of Violence and Trauma*,
DOI 10.1057/978-1-137-59445-7_6

at every turn; those imageries I know well enough—I grew up with them and am perhaps, to use Sontag's words, "anesthetized." What does affect me, however, in quite memorable ways is a singular, yet repetitive, moment when I find myself standing inside the space of what once functioned as a barrack for the prisoners at Auschwitz-Birkenau. There are traces of faint, large letters printed on the inside walls and my students ask me, each year, to translate those letters for them. *"Sei ruhig,"* reads one phrase, *"be quiet!"*, I translate. They are orders—cynical and cruel in that they discipline the prisoners in every aspect of their suffering while creating an illusion of some kind of normalcy in the camp wherein a following of those rules would somehow result in an end of their suffering, a way out. I can translate these orders because they are written in my native tongue; the language of the perpetrators.

The concept of haunting has been an exceptionally rewarding framework for illuminating the kinds of encounters my group of students and I have experienced over the years at sites that are witness to what Jameson so eloquently termed the "hurts of history."[1] "Haunting" has given us a language to apprehend and interpret our mental, emotional, and visceral experiences and to appreciate the transformative effect of those experiences—the very meaning of feeling haunted means that our encounters will stay with us long after the program's ending.

As an educator, haunting also conjured up ways to make visible to, and work through with, my students the methodologies of Holocaust representations at specific sites; the ways in which our learning is channeled through the so-called passage of absence[2]: We experience the absence produced by the Holocaust through certain sensory and material structures that translate memories of loss, hurt, and suffering for us.

Additionally, to take the concept of haunting seriously means to encourage and nourish in students the experience of "queer effects": that is to say, to recognize, and *name* the salient experience beyond what we only see and what we already know.[3] As such, the framework of haunting gives us permission to fold our encounters into a category of learning that meaningfully echo *both* history *and* subjective experiences, bodily affect *and* critical reflection.

All of this, I argue, is essential for an ethical encounter with and at sites: to allow oneself to be haunted and have a deep engagement with history to begin with; to engage in procedures of critical reflection that can attest to the ways in which we feel disrupted and affected in our physical and emotional comfort zone; to acknowledge the often involuntary nature of "secondary witnessing" and to accept the persistent presence of the traumatic effects—they may last; and finally, to "find a place for this experience" for which there may be no relief. Taken together, an ethical model for our gaze at the suffering of others and an ethical relationship with that history can be explored.

"*What was your main take-away from participating in this program?*"—a question, I ask my cohorts in a smaller group setting when we meet for a debrief session back on campus. A few months will have lapsed since we were on our five-week journey together; many spend their remaining weeks of summer at home with family and friends, working, traveling, or even taking part in another study abroad program. Three main responses stuck with me because of there are illustrative of the encounters narrated in these previous pages. One of the main "take-aways" speaks about the possibility and importance of making "personal connections"; here, students notice that their knowledge about the Holocaust transformed from *"being just history to feeling personally attached."* Students insist that this personal connection was exclusively made possible by "being there," being at the site. From there, many students described how the personal connection—a notion of "deeply caring"—opened up the possibility to grow in other areas; for instance, students report that it *"made me more interested in history,"* and that they developed an heightened awareness of urgencies today—neo-Nazism, racism, anti-Semitism. The last theme in responses had to do with the transmission of that personal knowledge. Here, students described the difficulty of *"how to integrate that knowledge when returning,"* mostly in relation to speaking with others about their experience. As one student poignantly reflected, *"the part that I took mostly away is also the part that I also could not explain to others."*

I began creating and leading this program from a place of hesitation, discomfort, and doubts about the possibility of an ethical engagement with the history of suffering and hurt of others at authentic sites. There was a sense of being caught between possibility and caution: between the allure of evoking an experience for my students without claiming to reenact someone else's suffering; between an authentic witnessing of the past and a staging or curating of one; between enabling a constructive confrontation with a painful past and the danger of traumatizing and paralyzing; between witnessing and simple gazing.

Each of the chapters in this book teased out one moment, or encounter, and highlights the problematic nature of such encounter as well as the possibilities and limits that exist within these encounters. Key debates in Holocaust education were consulted in that process, whereby a variety of discourses and disciplines were mediated. It makes sense to reiterate some of those discourses and a selection of the voices as they have been instrumental in negotiating my doubts and, thus, may inspire others to think through theirs. Much of the overall thinking in Chap. 1 about what "being there"—a visitor and witness to a site of trauma—consists of, and how we need to think critically about the kinds of expectations of/prior experiences of/and performances at/we bring to these places of suffering has been informed by the work of Elizabeth Dauphinee; her writings on the *Ethics of Researching War* provide a frank acknowledgment of the spectacle of academic consumption and elitist activities that researchers, scholars, teachers, travelers, and tourists alike engage in.[4] My students, too, "purchased the right to experience, to observe, and to witness."[5] How to mediate our "access" to sites and how to negotiate its effects was subsequently chronicled in Chap. 2 through the discourse of trauma, or dark, tourism. These doubts, therefore, had fundamentally to do with the roles and identities we take to sites of trauma and suffering.

My hesitation about the methodologies in our teaching about atrocities was at the core of the encounters narrated in Chap. 3. Here, the impetus for thinking critically about the graphic illustrations of violence—what images do and don't do; their affect on us; their representational efficacy; the alternatives to visual representations—has largely been shaped by the work of David Campbell and scholars friendly to his thinking about the politics of photography.[6] Campbell's work acted as a moral compass in my travels on how we appropriate Holocaust imagery for the purpose of teaching, and to what effect that may happen. Here, the ongoing debates on the pedagogical limits of using shocking atrocity footage were a valuable platform upon which to project the role and concept of horror and its visualization.

Moving on from Chap. 3, it was only a small step to take in beginning to think about the emotional affects of teaching at sites of trauma and violence. Jessica Auchter's contemporary take on the concept of haunting and being haunted provided a valuable outlet for communicating the kinds of bodily and sensory experiences that we encountered at the women's camp of Ravensbrück.[7] Chapter 4 traces how the representations of the Holocaust through the notion of absence and loss were perceived by students and how this perception, in turn, translated into contemplating the absence of women and gendered experiences in the teaching of the Holocaust overall.

The final encounter in Chap. 5 took cues from Marianne Hirsch's work on postmemory and the power of traumatic effects that we can experience when witnessing the suffering of an other.[8] Led by queries to what extent such vicarious experience may affect empathy and compassion, this chapter offers suggestions on how to create mechanisms for a safe and controlled teaching environment for students at sites.

While I began the journey with my students, as I said, with trepidations and hesitations, I have arrived at concluding that an ethical model for teaching at sites of trauma and violence can in fact exist. In seeking a more ethically astute experience, I would suggest, at a minimum, to foreground discussions and readings with students that explore the possible encounters of the kind described here (reading assignments, for instance, on the concept of trauma tourism). Just as important as ensuring that students understand the event and content of the Holocaust are prompting them to be aware of the debates sketched here, to critically confront their own role as spectators, and to query their own motivation for, and pleasure of, seeing "inhumanity close up."

BEING TOUCHED BY THE PAST

The queries weaving through the pages had their roots in the assumption that "being there" has to do with "seeing" close up. Here, the immediate question had to be the one that asks *why do we need to see?* And, what in fact do we see? The chapter on atrocity footage was particularly invested in qualifying the necessity of seeing and the tensions housed in debates on the merit of seeing—seeing atrocity, seeing suffering, seeing history. One of the main conclusions has ultimately to do with the fact that "being there" is *not* about seeing but about "being in"; I would argue that my overall observations gesture to the value of an absence of seeing—something I discussed in these pages via the concept of an aesthetics of absence—that made a significant impact on the students' experience. To recognize the absence of what once was, is productive elsewhere: in the experience of one's own performance in places that are marked by absence and that are now filled by one's presence. One of the most striking encounters for the students was the reflection on their ability to walk in and, more importantly, out of the gate that adorns the former Nazi camp at Auschwitz numerous times throughout a two-day stay adjacent to the former Nazi death camp. Something that those absent were not able to do.

In closing, I want to return to the concept of haunting and haunted-ness that provided such a rich modality by which I tried to understand the emotive aspects of this program. There is one particular feature of haunting that speaks to me as an educator and that I have introduced in Chap. 5: Gordon writes that haunting, unlike trauma, is distinctive for "producing a something-to-be-done."[9] In other words—it invites us to think about where to go from here. Gordon's sentiment beauti-fully resonates with another reflective piece of writing, *The Touch of the Past*, that engulfs what we term "pedagogical witnessing." The term sug-gests a public staging "and doing" of one's practices of reading, viewing, and listening that make evident "how witnessing may become an event in which an other's time may disrupt my own."[10] I am reminded of a deeply moving reflection paper that one of my students wrote in which she, I would argue, illustrates such a practice of witnessing that certainly left me, as an educator, in awe of the learning possibility of being there. The student writes in response to a personal connection she makes when seeing the memorial to the victims of euthanasia:

> For me, this memorial was so relevant because it gave me a new perspec-tive – a perspective that I can carry with me from now on throughout this trip and the rest of my life. This was so personally relevant because at all other memorials I have had feelings of humility and admiration, yet nowhere had I really felt fear. This fear challenged me and forced me to face the perspective that I thought would never be available to me.

My reflections on the current wisdom of Holocaust education have been inevitably long; I have spent more time identifying and sharpening the contours of the existing debates than offering solutions. This, however, should not come as a surprise; the encounters narrated here are per-sonal and subjective, and with that defy any attempts to offer universal paths for Holocaust education at sites. Having said that, throughout this book I provided some thought on how to mediate encounters at sites of trauma, and those were born out of the comments, feedback, and obser-vations with and of my students. Perhaps the title of another insight-ful resource, *Between Hope and Despair* is a fitting way to close this book.[11] The authors speak of our ongoing duty to provide possibilities to unsettle our frames of daily life, a task that ought to be "rooted in attempts to remain in relation with loss without being subsumed by it."[12] In order to achieve that, the teaching objectives encapsulated here had everything to do with critical learning and critical reflection resulting in a pedagogy that prepares students for a critical understanding of atrocity.

NOTES

1. Jameson, F. (1982) *The Political Unconscious: Narrative as a Socially Symbolic Act* (Ithaca, NY: Cornell University Press).
2. Heckner, E. (2008) "Whose Trauma is it?", in BAthrick, D., Prager, B. and Richardson, M. (Eds.) *Visualizing the Holocaust. Documents, Aesthetics, Memory,* (Rochester, NY: Camden House), p. 75.
3. Gordon, A. (1997) *Ghostly Matters,* (University of Minnesota Press), p. x.
4. Dauphinee, E. (2007) *The Ethics of Researching War. Looking for Bosnia* (Oxford University Press).
5. Dauphinee, *The Ethics of Researching War,* p. 38.
6. Campbell, D. (2004) "Horrific Blindness: Images of Death in Contemporary Media," *Journal for Cultural Research,* 8:1, 55–74.
7. Auchter, J. (2014) *The Politics of Haunting and Memory in International Relations* (Routledge).
8. Hirsch, M. (2001) "Surviving Images: Holocaust Photographs and the Work of Postmemory," *The Yale Journal of Criticism,* 14:1, 5–37.
9. Gordon, *Ghostly Matters,* p. xvi.
10. Simon, (2005) *The Touch of the Past. Remembrance, Learning and Ethics,* (Palgrave Macmillan), p. 107.
11. Simon, Simon, R., Rosenberg, S., and Eppert, C. (2000) *Between Hope and Despair* (Rowman & Littlefield).
12. Simon, Rosenberg, and Eppert, *Between Hope and Despair,* p. 5.

BIBLIOGRAPHY

Adelman, R. (2014) 'Atrocity and Aporiae: Teaching the Abu Ghraib Images, Teaching Against Transparency', *Cultural Studies and Critical Methodologies,* 12:1, 29–39.

Adelman, R. and Kozol, W. (2014) 'Discordant Affects: Ambivalence, Banality, and the Ethics of Spectatorship', *Theory & Event,* 17:3.

Alsup, J. (2003) 'A Pedagogy of Trauma', in Bernard-Donals, M. and Glejzer, R. (Eds.) *Witnessing the Disaster* (The University of Wisconsin Press), pp. 75–89.

Andrews, K., Gray, M. and Maws, A. (2013) 'Responses to B. J. Epstein's 'Inflicting Trauma', *Holocaust Studies: A Journal of Culture and History,* 19:1, 121–134.

Ashworth, G. (2002) 'Holocaust Tourism: The Experience of Krakow Kazimierz', *International Research in Geographical and Environmental Education,* 11·4, 363–367.

Ashworth, G. (2004) 'Tourism and the heritage of atrocity: Managing the heritage of South African apartheid for entertainment', in Singh, T. V. (Ed.) *New horizons in tourism: Strange experiences and stranger practices* (Basingstoke: CABI), pp. 95–108.

Ashwort, G. and Isaac, R. (2015) 'Have we illuminated the dark? Shifting perspectives on 'dark' tourism', *Tourism Recreation Research,* 40:3, 316–325.

Ashworth, G. and Hartman, R. (2005) *Horror and Human Tragedy revisited: The management of sites of atrocities for tourism,* (New York : Cognizant Communication Corporation).

Auchter, J. (2014) *The Politics of Haunting and Memory in International Relations* (Routledge).

Auschwitz-Birkenau News (2015) 'Growing attendance and security at the Memorial', Available: http://auschwitz.org/en/museum/news/

© The Editor(s) (if applicable) and The Author(s) 2018   83
N. Bormann, *The Ethics of Teaching at Sites of Violence and Trauma,*
DOI 10.1057/978-1-137-59445-7

growing-attendance-and-security-at-the-memorial,1147.html. Accessed 1 July 2016.

Auschwitz-Birkenau Museum News (2017) 'Over 2 million visitors at the Auschwitz Memorial in 2016' Available http://auschwitz.org/en/museum/news/over-2-million-visitors-at-the-auschwitz-memorial-in-2016,1232.html. Accessed 1 March 2017.

Bathrick, D. (2004) 'Teaching visual culture and the Holocaust', in Hirsch, M. and Kacandes, I. (Eds.) *Teaching the Representation of the Holocaust*, (New York: The Modern Language Association of America), pp. 286–300.

Bathrick, D., Prager, B. and Richardson, M., (Eds.) (2008) *Visualizing the Holocaust: Documents, Aesthetics, Memory* (Rochester, NY: Camden House).

Battani, M. (2011) 'Atrocity Aesthetics: Beyond Bodies and Compassion', *Afterimage* 39:1&2, 54–57.

Beech, J. (2000) 'The enigma of holocaust sites as tourist attractions—the case of Buchenwald', *Managing Leisure*, 5:1, 29–41.

Bleiker, R. (2015) 'Pluralist Methods for Visual Global Politics', *Millennium*, 43:3, 872–890.

Blum, L. (2004) 'The Poles, the Jews and the holocaust: reflections on an AME trip to Auschwitz', *Journal of Moral Education*, 33:2, 131–148.

Bönisch, J. (2010) 'Scheinheiliger Pflichtbesuch', *Süddeutsche Zeitung*, Available: http://www.sueddeutsche.de/karriere/nationalsozialismus-in-der-schule-scheinheiliger-pflichtbesuch-1.359663. Accessed 10 May 2017.

Bormann, N. (2016) 'The Importance of Remembering Nazi Perpetrators', *E-IR*, Available: http://www.e-ir.info/2016/09/14/the-importance-of-remembering-nazi-perpetrators/.

Bormann, N. and Czastkiewicz, V. (2017) '"Postcard from Auschwitz?": Chronicling the Challenges of a Holocaust Study Abroad Program', in Budryte, D. and Boykin, S. (Eds.) *Engaging Difference. Teaching Humanities and Social Science in Multicultural Environments*, (Rowman & Littlefield), pp. 111–120.

Brigg, M. and Blieker, R. (2010) 'Autoethnographic International Relations: exploring the self as a source of knowledge', *Review of International Studies*, 36, 779–798.

Brink C. (2000) 'Secular Icons: Looking at Photographs from Nazi Concentration Camps', *History & Memory* 12:1, 135–150.

Broder, H. (2014) 'Auschwitz ist heute ein Disneyland des Todes', *Die Welt* Available: https://www.welt.de/kultur/article124251623/Auschwitz-ist-heute-ein-Disneyland-des-Todes.html?config=print. Accessed 15 July 2015.

Brown, L. (2015) 'Memorials to the victims of Nazism: the impact on tourists in Berlin', *Journal of Tourism and Cultural Change*, 13:3, 244–260.

Brown, M. and Davies, I. (1998) 'The Holocaust and Education for Citizenship: the teaching of history, religion and human rights in England', *Educational*

Review, 50:1, 75–83. Gray, M. (2014) *Contemporary Debates in Holocaust Education*, (Palgrave Pivot).

Browning, C. (1992) *Ordinary Men: Reserve Police Battalion 101 and the Final Solution in Poland*, (Harper Perennial).

Buntman, B. (2008) 'Tourism and Tragedy: The Memorial at Belzec, Poland', *International Journal of Heritage Studies*, 14:5, 422–448.

Callahan, W. (2015) 'The Visual Turn in IR: Documentary Filmmaking as a Critical Method', *Millennium*, 43:3, 891–910.

Campbell, D. (2002) 'Atrocity, memory, photography: Imaging the concentration camps of Bosnia–the case of ITN versus Living Marxism, Part 1', *Journal of Human Rights*, 1:2, 143–172.

Campbell, D. (2004) 'Horrific blindness: Images of Death in Contemporary Media', *Journal for Cultural Research*, 8:1, 55–74.

Campbell, D. (2011) 'Thinking Images v.21: Seeing the Dead'. Available: https://www.david-campbell.org/2011/08/30/thinking-images-v-21-seeing-the-dead/. Accessed 10 May 2013.

Carruthers, S. (2001) 'Compulsory Viewing: Concentration Camp Film and German Re-education' *Millennium* 30:3, 733–759.

Cavarero, A. (2008) *Horrorism: Naming Contemporary Violence*, (Columbia University Press).

Clyde, C. (2010) 'Developing civic leaders through an experiential learning programme for Holocaust education', *Prospects*, 40, 289–306.

Clyde, C., Walker, D. and Floyd, D. (2005) 'An Experiential Learning Program for Holocaust Education', *Journal of Student Affairs Research and Practice*, 42:3, 37–41.

Cole, T. (1999) *Selling the Holocaust—From Auschwitz to Schindler: How History is bought, packaged, and sold*, (New York: Routledge).

Cowan, P. and Maitles, H. (2010) 'We saw inhumanity close up', *Journal of Curriculum Studies*, 43:2, 163–184.

Dachau Museum and Memorial Site 'Is the memorial site appropriate for children', Available: https://www.kz-gedenkstaette-dachau.de/frequently-asked-questionsfaq/items/is-the-memorial-site-appropriate-for-children-9.html. Accessed 3 March 2017.

Dachau Museum and Memorial Site 'Notes on the Documentary film 'The Dachau Concentration Camp 1933–1945'. Available https://www.kz-gedenkstaette-dachau.de/documentary_film.html. Accessed 1 May 2016.

Dauphinee, E. (2007) *The Ethics of Researching War. Looking for Bosnia*, (Oxford University Press).

Dauphinee, E. (2007) 'The politics of the body in pain: Reading the ethics of imagery', *Security Dialogue*, 38, 139–155.

Dauphinee, E. (2010) 'The ethics of autoethnography', *Review of International Studies*, 36, 799–818.

Dekel, I. (2009) 'Ways of looking: Observation and transformation at the Holocaust Memorial, Berlin', *Memory Studies,* 2:1, 71–86.

Dewey, J. (1938) *Experience and Education,* (New York: MacMillan).

Edkins, J. (2004) 'Ground Zero: Reflections on Trauma, In/Distinction and Response', *Journal for Cultural Research,* 8:3, 247–270.

Ezra, E. (2014) 'A Pedagogy of Empathy for a World of Atrocity', *Review of Education, Pedagogy, and Cultural Studies,* 36:5, 343–371.

Felman, S. (1991) 'In an era of testimony: Shoah', *Yale French Studies,* 79, 39–81.

Foley, M. and Lennon, J. (1997) 'Dark Tourism—An Ethical Dilemma', in Foley, M. Lennon, J. and Maxwell, G. (Eds.) *Strategic Issues for the Hospitality, Tourism and Leisure Industries,* (London: Cassell), pp. 153–64.

Foley, M. and McPherson, G. (2010) 'Museums as Leisure', *International Journal of Heritage Studies,* 6:2, 161–174.

Gilbert, M. (1999) *Holocaust Journey,* (Columbia University Press).

Golanska, D. (2015) 'AffectiveSspaces, Sensuous Engagements: In Quest of a Synaestethic Approach to 'Dark Memorials', *International Journal of Heritage Studies* 21 (8): 773–790.

Goldhagen, D. (1975) *Hitler's Willing Executioners* (Alfred Knopf).

Gordon, A. (2008) *Ghostly Matters: Haunting and the Sociological Imagination,* (Minneapolis, MN: University of Minnesota Press).

Gray, M. (2014) *Contemporary Debates in Holocaust Education,* (UK: Palgrave MacMillan).

Hall, T. and Ross, A. (2015) 'Affective Politics after 9.11', *International Organization,* May, 1–33.

Hartmann, R. (2014) 'Dark tourism, thanatourism, and dissonance in heritage tourism management: new directions in contemporary tourism research, *Journal of Heritage Journalism* 9:2, 166–182.

Harvey, E. (2009) 'Women as perpetrators', Conference Contribution *Perpetrator Research in a Global Context,* Available: http://www.bpb.de/veranstaltungen/dokumentation/127465/perpetrator-research-in-a-global-context-taeterforschung-im-globalen-kontext. Accessed 15 May 2015.

Heckner, E. (2008) 'Whose Trauma is it?', In Bathrick, D., Prager, B. and Richardsen, M. (Eds.) *Visualizing the Holocaust. Documents, Aesthetics, Memory,* (New York: Camden House), pp. 62–85.

Heyl, M. (1997) *Erziehung nach Auschwitz. Eine Bestandsaufnahme,* (Kraemer Verlag).

Heyl, M. (2009) 'Teaching and Learning about Perpetrators within Memorial Sites', Conference Contribution *Perpetrator Research in a Global Context,* Available: http://www.bpb.de/veranstaltungen/dokumentation/127465/perpetrator-research-in-a-global-context-taeterforschung-im-globalen-kontext. Accessed 15 May 2015.

Hirsch, M. (2001) 'Surviving Images: Holocaust Photographs and the Work of Postmemory', *The Yale Journal of Criticism*, 14:1, 5–37.

Hirsch, M. and Kacandes, I. (2004) *Teaching the Representation of the Holocaust*, (New York: The Modern Language Association of America).

Jameson, F. (1982) *The Political Unconscious: Narrative as a Socially Symbolic Act*, (Ithaca, NY: Cornell University Press).

Jeffries, S. (2015) 'The Holocaust Film that was too shocking to show', *The Guardian*. Avialable https://www.theguardian.com/film/2015/jan/09/holocaust-film-too-shocking-to-show-night-will-fall-alfred-hitchcock. Accessed 12 June, 2015.

Johnson, J. (2011) 'The Arithmetic of Compassion': Rethinking the Politics of Photography', *British Journal of Political Science*, 41:3, 621–643.

Kansteiner, W. (2014) 'Genocide memory, digital cultures, and the aesthetization of violence', *Memory Studies* 7:4, 403–408.

Kaplan, B. A. (2011) *Landscapes of Holocaust Postmemory*, (New York and London: Routledge).

Kranz, T. (2013) *The Pedagogy of Remembrance as a Form of Museum Education*.

Clyde, C. (2010) 'Developing civic leaders through an experiential learning programme for Holocaust education', *Prospect*, 40, 289–306.

Kranz, T. (2013) *Educational Visits to the State Museum at Majdanek—A Guide for Teachers*, (Lublin: Państwowe Muzeum na Majdanku).

Landsberg, A. (2004) *Prosthetic Memory: The Age of Transformation of American Remembrance in the Age of Mass Culture*, (Columbia University Press), p. 130.

Lennon, J., and Foley, M. (2000) *Dark tourism: The attraction of death and disaster*, (New York, NY: Continuum).

Lezra, E. (2014) 'A Pedagogy of Empathy for a World of Atrocity', *The Review of Education, Pedagogy and Cultural Studies* 36, 343–371.

Linfield, S. (2001) 'Beyond the Sorrow and the Pity', *Dissent* 48;1, 100–106, p. 104.

Littell, J. (2006) *The Kindly Ones*, (HarperCollins).

Lukianoff, G. and Haidt, J. (2015) 'The Coddling of the American Mind', *The Atlantic*, Available: https://www.theatlantic.com/magazine/archive/2015/09/the-coddling-of-the-american-mind/399356/. Accessed 20 March 2016.

Margalit, R. (2014) 'Should Auschwitz be a site for selfies?', *The New Yorker* Available: http://www.newyorker.com/culture/culture-desk/should-auschwitz-be-a-site-for-selfies. Accessed 1 July 2014.

Mazza, E. (2015) 'Auschwitz summer cooling 'showers' angers visitors', *The Huffington Post* Available: http://www.huffingtonpost.com/entry/auschwitz-showers_us_55e55415e4b0aec9f3546077. Accessed 10 October 2015.

Nawijn, J. and Fricke, M.-C. (2015) 'Visitor Emotions and Behavioral Intentions: The Case of Concentration Camp Memorial Neuengamme, *International Journal of Tourism Research*, 17:3, 221–228.

Payne, E. (2015) 'Auschwitz becomes the world's most unlikely tourist hot spot', *Daily Mail UK Online* Available: http://www.dailymail.co.uk/travel/travel_news/article-3052542/So-popular-turning-people-away-Auschwitz-world-s-unlikely-tourist-hot-spot-40-increase-visitors.html. Accessed 1 March 2017.

Prager, B. (2008) 'On the Liberation of Perpetrator Photographs in Holocaust Narratives', in Bathrick, D., Prager, B. and Richardson, M. (Eds.) *Visualizing the Holocaust*, (Rochester, New York: Camden House), pp. 19–37.

Romi, S., and Lev, M. (2007) 'Experiential learning of history through youth journeys to Poland: Israeli Jewish youth and the holocaust', *Research in Education*, 78, 88–102.

Schechter, H. and Salomon, P. (2005) 'Does vicarious experience of suffering affect empathy for an adversary? The effects of Israelis' visits to Auschwitz on their empathy for Palestinians', *Journal of Peace Research*, 2:2, 125–138.

Seaton, A. V. (1996) 'Guided by the dark: From thanatopsis to thanatourism', *International Journal of Heritage Studies* 2:4, 234–244.

Seaton, A. (2009) 'Purposeful Otherness: Approaches to the management of thanatourism', in Sharpley, R. and Stone, P. (Eds.) *The Darker Side of Travel*, (Bristol: Channel View Publications), pp. 75–108.

Selzer, M. (1997) 'Wound Culture: Trauma in the Pathological Public Sphere', *October* 80: Spring, 3–26.

Sharply, R. (2009) 'Shedding Light on Dark Tourism', in Sharply and Stone, *The Darker Side of Travel*, pp. 3–22.

Sharpley R. (2012) 'Towards and understanding of "Genocide Tourism": an analysis of visitors' accounts of their experience of recent genocide sites', in Sharpley, R. and Stone, P. (Eds.) *Contemporary Tourist Experience: Concepts and Consequences* (Abingdon: Routledge), pp. 95–109.

Sharpley, R. (2016) 'Death Tourism: Disaster Sites as Recreational Landscapes. Book Review', *Journal of Policy Research in Tourism, Leisure and Events*, 8:3, 342–344.

Simon, R. (2005) *The touch of the past. Remembrance, Learning, and Ethics*, (Palgrave Macmillan).

Simon, Simon, R., Rosenberg, S., and Eppert, C. (2000) *Between Hope and Despair*, (Rowman & Littlefield).

Simon, R. and Eppert, C. (2005) 'Remembering obligation: witnessing testimonies of historical trauma', in Simon, R. (ed) *The Touch of the Past. Remembrance, Learning and Ethics*, (Palgrave MacMillan), pp. 50–64.

Sion, B. (Ed.) (2014) *Death Tourism: Disaster Sites as Recreational Landscape*, (London; New York; Calcutta: Seagull Books).

Smith, V. (1998) 'War and Tourism: An American Ethnography', *Annals of Tourism Research*, 25, 202–227.

Smith, S. (2007) 'Teaching about the Holocaust in the setting of museums and memorials', in Goldenberg, M. and Millen, R. (Eds.) *Testimony, Tension, and Tikkun*, (University of Washington Press), 271–283.

Sontag, S. (2003) *Regarding the Pain of Others*, (Farrar, Straus and Giroux).

Stone, P. (2006) 'A Dark Tourism Spectrum: Towards a Typology of Death and Macabre Related Tourist Sites, Attractions and Exhibitions', *Tourism*, 54:2, 145–160, p. 146.

Stone, P. (2009) *'The Darker Side of Travel*, (Channel View Publications).

Stone, P. and Sharpley, R. (2008) 'Consuming dark tourism: A thanatological perspective', *Annals of Tourism Research*, 35:2, 574–595.

The European Union Agency for Fundamental Rights (2011) *Excursion to the Past—Teaching for the Future: Handbook for Teachers* Available: http://fra.europa.eu/en/publication/2010/excursion-past-teaching-future-handbook-teachers. Accessed 10 March 2014.

Totten, S. (2002) *Holocaust Education: Issues and Approaches*, (Boston: Allyn and Bacon).

Totten, S. and Feinberg, S. (2001) *Teaching and Studying the Holocaust*, (Boston: Allyn and Bacon).

Trigg, D. (2009) 'The place of trauma: Memory, hauntings, and the temporality of ruins', *Memory Studies*, 2:1, 87–101.

Thurnell-Read, T. (2009) 'Engaging Auschwitz: an analysis of young travellers' experiences of Holocaust tourism', *Journal of Tourism Consumption and Practice* 1(1): 26–52.

Wollaston, I. (2005) 'Negotiating the marketplace: The role(s) of Holocaust museums today', *Journal of Modern Jewish Studies*, 4.1, 63–80.

Wysok, W. (2013) 'The principles of cooperation between museum pedagogical staff at memorial sites and teachers in carrying out educational projects – practical remarks', in Thomas Kranz et al (Eds.) *The Purpose of Visiting Sties of Trauma in Education*.

Young, J. (1993) *The texture of memory*, (Yale University Press).

Young, J. (2016) 'The memorial's arc: Between Berlin's Denkmal and New York City's 9/11 Memorial', *Memory Studies*, 9:3, 325–331.

Zeitlin, F. (2004) 'Teaching about Perpetrators', in Hirsch, M. and Kacandes, I. (Eds.) *Teaching the Representation of the Holocaust* (New York: Modern Language Association of America).

INDEX

© The Editor(s) (if applicable) and The Author(s) 2018   91
N. Bormann, *The Ethics of Teaching at Sites of Violence and Trauma*,
DOI 10.1057/978-1-137-59445-7

CPSIA information can be obtained
at www.ICGtesting.com
Printed in the USA
BVOW06*0214260917
495920BV00004B/29/P